ROMAN BRITAIN

by R. R. Sellman

Illustrated by the Author and
ALAN SORRELL

ROY PUBLISHERS, INC. NEW YORK

First published in 1956
Third edition 1963
© 1959 R. R. Sellman
Library of Congress Catalogue Card No. 63-18302
Printed in Great Britain

Contents

The Road Builders.

(*See p. 40.*)

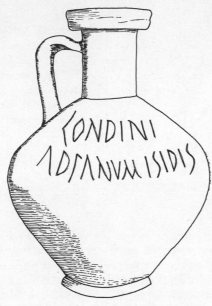

Inscribed jug from Southwark: "Londini ad Fanum Isidis"—
"At London, at the Temple of Isis."

INTRODUCTION: THE EVIDENCE

No part of British history has been so sweepingly re-written in the last fifty years as that of Roman Britain. The surviving written records of Roman times, on which earlier historians mostly relied, give little more than a brief and sometimes misleading outline of the achievements of Emperors and Generals. They have little or nothing of value to say on the civilisation of Britain before the Roman Conquest, and the extent to which it was "Romanised" afterwards, or on what really happened in that dim period when Roman Britain gave way to Saxon England.

Nothing final on these subjects can yet be said, but immense progress has been made in recent years towards a clearer understanding of those four centuries when Britain was a Province of Imperial Rome. This progress is the work of a host of archaeologists, experts of our national museums, and enthusiastic (and not inexpert) amateurs of our local societies. The spade—and on occasion the teaspoon and toothbrush—have revealed a mass of detailed evidence which the historian can now put together like an enormous jig-saw puzzle. Many pieces are yet missing, and some do not quite fit, but the general picture is becoming clear.

Modern scientific excavation, which carefully distinguishes the different layers of a site, can reconstruct the history of a

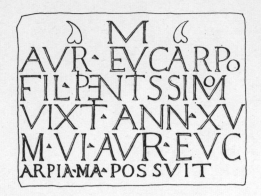

Memorial to a Roman boy, found in London. "Marco Aurelio Eucarpo, filio pientissimo, vixit annos XV menses VI, Aurelia Eucarpia mater possuit"—To Marcus Aurelius Eucarpus, most dutiful son, who lived fifteen years and six months, his mother Aurelia set up (this monument).

town, a villa, or a village, and find when it was built, rebuilt or enlarged, was flourishing or decayed, and when (and sometimes how) it was finally destroyed or abandoned. It can also tell, from the style of the buildings and the objects found in them, how far the inhabitants adopted the Roman way of life. Excavation of forts and defences likewise builds up the military history of the Province, and of the outside threats and attacks which eventually caused its fall. When such evidence from a great number of sites is put together, we can produce a connected history of Roman Britain as a whole.

Apart from the actual plans of buildings revealed by digging, a great variety of finds may help to reconstruct the story. Inscriptions record the date of military and public buildings, and the name of the unit, Governor, or local authority responsible. Inscribed altars give the name of the god to whom they were dedicated and of the individual or group who set them up, and tombstones tell us about individuals and troop movements. Milestones,

giving the name of the current Emperor and the distance to the nearest town or fort, show when roads were built or repaired and help to fix the names of places. Stamps on metal pigs help with the dating and distribution of industry; and personal messages scratched on wet tiles or plaster show how far ordinary people could read and write in Latin.

Coins are a sign of trade and outside contacts, and from their dates and frequency we can reasonably guess how long

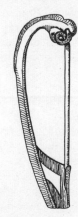

Bronze "safety-pin" brooch used for fastening clothing.

2

a place was inhabited and how Romanised was its life. If there are far more of one period than of others, we can infer when it was most populated and prosperous: and if hoards of coins ending in a particular date are found hidden all over the country we may assume a time of insecurity and danger.

Pottery gives similar information. Imported wares like the Gaulish "Samian", and mass-produced pots from the main British potteries, indicate a Romanised way of life, and their shapes and styles give good evidence for dating. Tools and weapons (or lack of them), and articles of dress and ornament, contribute to the picture of daily life: and the skeletons of

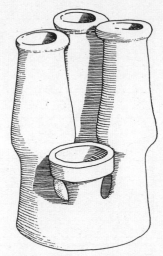

Multiple flower-vase, found near Newgate, London.

the inhabitants tell us something of their physical type, and sometimes how they died.

At Lullingstone in Kent, fragments of coloured plaster have recently revealed a room apparently fitted up as a villa-chapel, with walls covered with unmistakably Christian paintings.

Every year fresh material comes to light. Photographs from aircraft in a dry season reveal the lines of foundations and roads invisible on the ground (from the lighter shade of the grass above them); and clearance or war-time bombing have allowed the digging of areas normally covered by town buildings. The writer of fifty years hence will tell a much fuller, and perhaps a rather different, story: but he is not likely to differ so completely from the ideas of the present day as we do from those of fifty years ago.

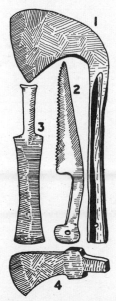

Carpenter's tools from Roman London: 1, axe-head; 2, saw-blade; 3, chisel; 4, axe-hammer.

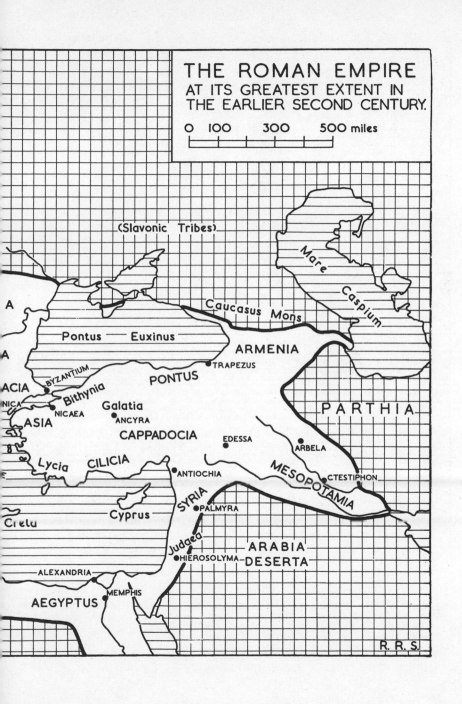

THE ROMAN EMPIRE
AT ITS GREATEST EXTENT IN
THE EARLIER SECOND CENTURY.

0   100   300   500 miles

(Slavonic Tribes)

Mare Caspium

Caucasus Mons

Pontus — Euxinus

ARMENIA

TRAPEZUS

A

PONTUS

BYZANTIUM

Bithynia

Galatia

NICAEA

ANCYRA

PARTHIA

ACIA

NICA

ASIA

CAPPADOCIA

EDESSA

ARBELA

Lycia

CILICIA

ANTIOCHIA

MESOPOTAMIA

CTESIPHON

Cyprus

SYRIA

PALMYRA

Creta

Judaea

ARABIA
DESERTA

HIEROSOLYMA

ALEXANDRIA

MEMPHIS

AEGYPTUS

R. R. S.

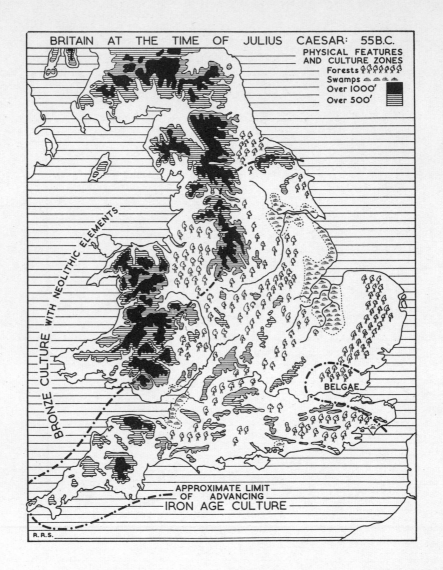

BRITAIN AT THE TIME OF JULIUS CAESAR· 55 B.C.

PHYSICAL FEATURES AND CULTURE ZONES

Forests
Swamps
Over 1000'
Over 500'

BRONZE CULTURE WITH NEOLITHIC ELEMENTS

BELGAE

APPROXIMATE LIMIT OF ADVANCING IRON AGE CULTURE

R.R.S.

BRITAIN AT THE TIME OF JULIUS CAESAR

Britain was, and still is, divided geographically into two distinct zones—the Lowlands of the Midlands and South and the Highlands of the South-West, Wales, and the North. This distinction is still important; but in ancient times, when

6

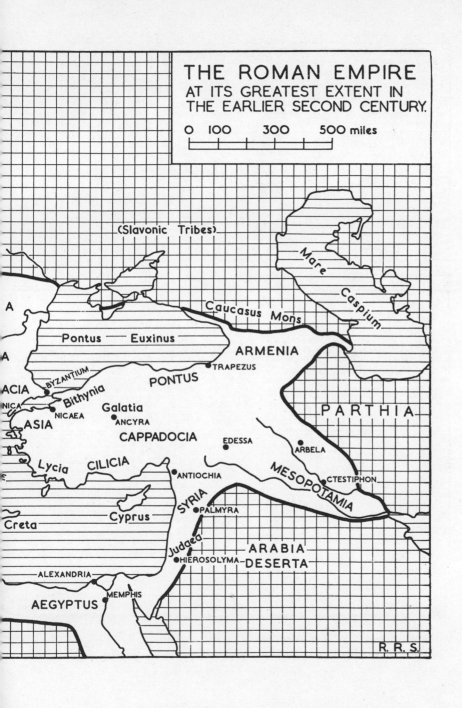

THE ROMAN EMPIRE
AT ITS GREATEST EXTENT IN THE EARLIER SECOND CENTURY.

0   100   300   500 miles

(Slavonic Tribes)

Mare Caspium

Caucasus Mons

Pontus — Euxinus

ARMENIA

TRAPEZUS

A

A

ACIA

BYZANTIUM

NICA

Bithynia

PONTUS

PARTHIA

ASIA

NICAEA

Galatia

ANCYRA

CAPPADOCIA

EDESSA

ARBELA

Lycia

CILICIA

ANTIOCHIA

MESOPOTAMIA

CTESTIPHON

Creta

Cyprus

SYRIA

PALMYRA

Judaea

ARABIA
DESERTA

HIEROSOLYMA

ALEXANDRIA

AEGYPTUS

MEMPHIS

R. R. S.

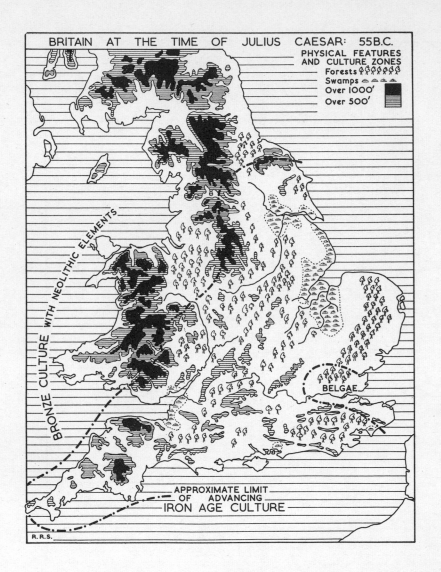

BRITAIN AT THE TIME OF JULIUS CAESAR: 55B.C.
PHYSICAL FEATURES AND CULTURE ZONES
Forests
Swamps
Over 1000'
Over 500'

BRONZE CULTURE WITH NEOLITHIC ELEMENTS

BELGAE

APPROXIMATE LIMIT OF ADVANCING IRON AGE CULTURE

R.R.S.

BRITAIN AT THE TIME OF JULIUS CAESAR

Britain was, and still is, divided geographically into two distinct zones—the Lowlands of the Midlands and South and the Highlands of the South-West, Wales, and the North. This distinction is still important; but in ancient times, when

6

men were much more dependent for their way of life on the country they lived in, it mattered far more. The Highland zone, with its plateaus and mountains, has changed little except where men have built settlements: but the Lowlands have been altered out of all recognition.

The people of the Lowland zone before and during the Roman occupation lived mostly on the well-drained chalk and limestone hills, where the soil was too thin to support forests and where cultivable land could be had by burning off the grass and scrub. The valleys, where most live today, had their heavy clay soils covered with wolf-infested forests or with marsh, and they were avoided. There was no point in clearing the lower ground, which in any case was too heavy for the light wheel-less plough which sufficed on the hills, and the ridges were easier to move about on and easier to fortify against the attacks of men or beasts.

Only in the extreme south-east was there an exception to this rule. Here tribes of a people called the Belgae, from the other side of the Channel, had settled about 75 B.C., and had brought with them a heavy wheeled plough capable of dealing with clay. In East Kent and round the Thames Estuary they were already clearing trees and breaking up the more fertile valley soils, and establishing isolated farms in forest clearings. The Belgae were a vigorous and warlike people, and sufficiently advanced to make their own coins.

Beyond their settlements stretched the upland villages of powerful tribes using iron and bronze—the Trinovantes, Iceni, and Regni—as far as the Wiltshire hills, the Midland forests, and the Fens. These people built hill-forts as refuges, and some of their villages were large enough to be recognised as "capitals". Westwards and northwards still, the people, if more primitive, were still organised in strong kingdoms; and some of them produced works of art in the form of abstract curved designs on metal, which are of remarkable quality.

Over all the Lowland zone iron was in common use, clothing of wool or linen was worn, and life was organised in farming villages knit together by allegiance to a powerful tribal king. People here were far from the blue-painted savages of some history books. In the Highland zone, however, iron had penetrated little: bronze was still the chief metal, and its expensiveness meant that most people still had to depend on wood and stone for tools and weapons. Here too the organisation was tribal, but poorer tools and soils meant a lower standard of living.

THE ROMAN EMPIRE

Meanwhile, around the shores of the Mediterranean there had been growing up an Empire unique in the history of the world. Starting as one small Italian city, by superior military organisation and ability in government and engineering Rome had made herself mistress of the Mediterranean world. In the arts of peace she learnt much from Greece (which became part of her Empire) but in those of war she required no instructor.

The Legions of citizen-soldiers, each containing some 5,000–5,500 infantry and a small force of cavalry, made and garrisoned her conquests. Their discipline and organisation gave them mastery over much greater numbers, and their engineers

7

COMMON ROMAN WEAPONS

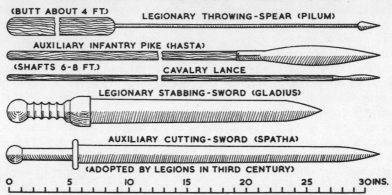

(BUTT ABOUT 4 FT.) LEGIONARY THROWING-SPEAR (PILUM)

AUXILIARY INFANTRY PIKE (HASTA)

(SHAFTS 6-8 FT.) CAVALRY LANCE

LEGIONARY STABBING-SWORD (GLADIUS)

AUXILIARY CUTTING-SWORD (SPATHA)

(ADOPTED BY LEGIONS IN THIRD CENTURY)

0   5   10   15   20   25   30INS.

The legionary threw the Pilum to disorder an enemy's ranks immediately before charging in with the Gladius. Its heavy wooden butt gave it force, and its long thin soft-iron shaft was designed to bend on impact so that it could not be thrown back.

and masons laid out the roads and built the forts which held down the conquered provinces. In weapons, apart from their stone- and spear-throwing artillery, they had no great advantage: the short stabbing-sword and throwing-spears could be equalled by their iron-using enemies. But their armour and large shields made them much less vulnerable, and their discipline ensured an unbroken front in defence or attack. Against ramparts and stockades they could form the "tortoise" of shields completely covering the front ranks from above as well as from the sides, and allowing others a foothold from which to scale the defences.

The peoples they conquered had no modern ideas of nationalism and independence, and were quite ready for the most part to settle down after a time and regard themselves as "Romans". The only exception was the Jews, who rebelled so fiercely and repeatedly that they had to be dispersed. To the civilised peoples of the eastern Mediterranean, Rome brought the blessings of peace which they had never enjoyed under their previous rulers; and to the tribal societies of northern and western Europe she offered also the attractions of a higher civilisation.

Before long the conquered began themselves to serve in the Roman armies, and the business of the Legions became the defence of the borders of the Empire rather than the suppression of revolts inside it. From most of the provinces men were recruited as Auxiliaries, in infantry Cohorts or cavalry Alae 500 or 1,000 strong, lighter armed than the Legionaries and often retaining their native bows or slings. While the Legions remained the backbone of the Army, the Auxiliaries were better suited for the patrol of frontiers and for dealing with minor raids.

A wise precaution moved them out of the province in which they were originally raised, but once they (like the Legions) settled down permanently it was not long before they married locally and recruited on the spot. On retirement after twenty-five years' service, the Auxiliary received full Roman citizenship.

From Syria to Spain, on both sides of the Mediterranean, there was no frontier and no consciousness of separate nationality: Latin served everywhere (though other languages, particularly Greek, continued to be spoken) and one system of roads and coinage linked all Romans together. By the time of Julius Caesar, "Romans" were no longer necessarily Italians: Spaniards, Africans, Gauls, Greeks, and many others shared the name of Rome.

JULIUS CAESAR'S INVASIONS

During the years 58–55 B.C., Julius Caesar conquered Gaul. He was building up a reputation and an armed following which he could later use in a bid for the Dictatorship, and he published his exploits in his famous *Commentaries* from which comes most of our knowledge of his invasions of Britain. The Britons,

like the Gauls, were Celts, similar in speech and way of life, connected by trade and religion, and in some cases (like the Belgae) having close tribal ties with the other side of the Channel. Caesar apparently found the Britons supporting his enemies in Gaul, and resolved to teach them a sharp lesson.

In 55 B.C. he made a reconnaissance in force, with two Legions and Auxiliaries, and fought his way ashore at Deal. The Kentish chiefs were at first overawed into submission, but when his carelessly beached or anchored ships were partly destroyed in a gale they prepared to fight again. The position was untenable: for a time he was without transport or supplies, and as soon as he could repair his least damaged ships from the wreckage of the rest he sailed back to Boulogne. As a reconnaissance, this was hardly successful: he had his first experience of British war-chariots, but completely failed to find the sheltered harbour a few miles away at Richborough which would have saved the disaster to his ships on this and the following occasion.

The following year he made his real effort, with five Legions and a great fleet of specially built transports. Landing

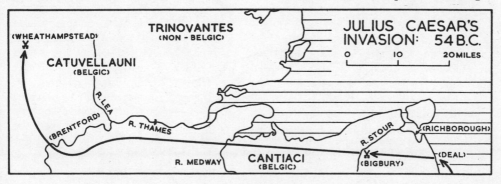

again near Deal, this time unopposed, he marched straight inland to bring the Britons to battle. At Bigbury, near Canterbury, the Legionaries stormed the stockades of a hill-fort; but again a gale damaged his fleet and he had to return and beach it above high-water mark and protect it with palisades and troops.

The Belgae of Kent called in the aid of their compatriot Cassivellaunus, chief of the Catuvellauni, whose capital lay at Wheathampstead near St. Albans. But they still could not halt the Legions. The line of the Medway was not defended, and Caesar reached the Thames and crossed it near Brentford. Chariots harassed his march and his foraging parties, but they could not break the embattled lines of the Legions and could themselves be driven off by a determined charge of Auxiliary cavalry.

The Trinovantes, a non-Belgic tribe who had an old score against Cassivellaunus, then submitted to Caesar and were happy to see the Legionaries storm their enemy's capital. It seemed that nothing could stop a victorious career of conquest across the island.

But in leaving Gaul, Caesar had taken the larger part of his army from that newly conquered province; and once he was gone the Gauls, led by Vercingetorix, prepared to rebel. Caesar had no alternative but to pull out and re-cross the Channel; it was useless to conquer Britain if meanwhile a successful revolt in Gaul should cut him off from Rome. Not to return quite empty-handed, he made terms with Cassivellaunus to the effect that the Catuvellauni were to pay annual tribute to Rome, give hostages, and leave the Trinovantes alone. But only a Roman army on the spot could have enforced the terms, and Caesar was soon far

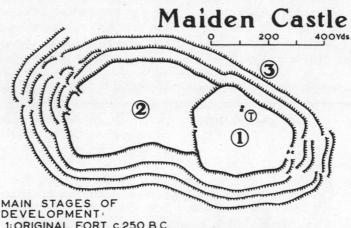

Maiden Castle

0   200   400 Yds.

MAIN STAGES OF
DEVELOPMENT:
1: ORIGINAL FORT c.250 B.C.
 (OVERLYING NEOLITHIC CAUSEWAYED CAMP c.2400 B.C.)
2: EXTENSION c.150 B.C.   3: OUTER RAMPARTS c.50 B.C.
Ⓣ - ROMAN TEMPLE AND PRIEST'S HOUSE c.370 A.D.

DOMINANT TRIBAL KINGDOMS c. 40 A.D.

BRIGANTES

CORNOVII

CORITANI

(Fens)

ICENI

SILURES

DOBUNI

CIRENCESTER

EASTERN BELGAE (CUNOBELINUS)

COLCHESTER

SILCHESTER

WESTERN BELGAE

(Weald Forest)

R. R. S.

too busy elsewhere to spare forces for Britain.

Caesar's invasion came too soon after his conquest of Gaul. Britain could not be conquered until Gaul was peaceful and secure—but once Gaul was pacified the way was open.

BRITAIN BEFORE THE ROMAN CONQUEST

For nearly a century the threat of conquest hung over Britain, but somehow the storm failed to break. The Emperors, who had now replaced the former republican government, sometimes talked of, and even prepared for, conquest; but always something happened to draw their attention elsewhere.

Meanwhile, Britain was not standing still. After Vercingetorix's rebellion in Gaul was crushed, a new wave of Belgae crossed to Britain, established themselves in Hampshire and Berkshire, and spread into neighbouring Surrey, Sussex, Wiltshire and Dorset. These people, called Atrebates, founded a capital at Silchester and struck coins like the other Belgae. They also marked their borders with a line of immense hill-forts, which they built or captured, of which Maiden Castle near Dorchester is the outstanding example. (See page 10.)

TIME-CHART OF ROMAN BRITAIN

A.D.	LOWLANDS	UPLANDS
	ROMAN INFLUENCE IN SOUTH-EAST.	
—50—	43: **Roman Invasion** CONQUEST OF LOWLANDS: MAIN ROADS BUILT. 61: BOUDICCA'S REVOLT.	61: PENETRATION OF NORTH WALES. 71-4: WAR WITH BRIGANTES. 78-84: **Conquests of Agricola.**
	Civil Organisation. ROMANISED TOWNS.	DEFENSIVE CONSOLIDATION.
—100—		
	DEVELOPMENT OF VILLAS	122: **Hadrian's Wall.** GROWTH OF WELSH AND PICTISH HILL-FORTS. 142: ANTONINE WALL.
—150—	MAXIMUM GROWTH OF TOWNS.	154: REVOLT OF BRIGANTES.
		ANTONINE WALL ABANDONED. 196: ALBINUS WITHDRAWS TROOPS: HADRIAN'S WALL WRECKED.
—200—		SEVERUS REBUILDS HADRIAN'S WALL AND INVADES SCOTLAND.
—250—	CRISIS AND DECLINE IN IMPERIAL GOVERNMENT: DECAY OF TOWNS.	REVIVAL OF CORNISH TIN-MINES.
	SAXON PIRACY BEGINS. 287-295: GOVERNMENT OF CARAUSIUS.	
—300—	**Saxon Shore Defences.** SPREAD OF CHRISTIANITY.	296: PICTISH ATTACKS RECOMMENCE. IRISH RAIDS INTENSIFIED.
—350—	DEPRESSION OF PEASANTRY: PROSPERITY OF VILLAS AND WOOLLEN INDUSTRY.	IRISH SETTLEMENT IN WEST.
	368: BRITAIN OVERRUN BY PICTS, IRISH, AND SAXONS.	COASTAL SIGNAL STATIONS. 383: MAXIMUS WITHDRAWS TROOPS: HADRIAN'S WALL ABANDONED.
—400—	STILICHO REORGANISES DEFENCES: UPLANDS LEFT TO FOEDERATI. MOST REMAINING TROOPS WITHDRAWN.	
	410: **Rescript of Honorius.** TEMPORARY REOCCUPATION OF SOUTH-EAST? ECLIPSE OF ROMANISED CLASS: RISE OF 'TYRANTS'.	CHRISTIAN MISSIONS IN SOUTHERN SCOTLAND AND WALES.
—450—	**Saxon Settlement in South-East.**	

Other tribes also began to strike coins, and from the evidence of their issues we can trace kingdoms of the Iceni in East Anglia, of the Dobuni in the Cotswolds and Upper Thames, and the Brigantes in the north. These kingdoms, with that of Cunobelinus (successor of Cassivellaunus) in the south-east, seem to have partitioned most of Lowland Britain between them, though other tribes continued to exist as tributaries.

With the spread of coinage, and therefore of trade, south-east Britain was coming into closer contact with the Empire. Corn and cattle, iron, hides, and slaves are listed among her exports, and Roman pottery and metalwork were being imported. The wealthier classes were already showing an interest in the material side of Roman life, and (as happened in later history) the Roman merchant was preparing the way for the soldier.

THE CONQUEST OF BRITAIN

In A.D. 43 Rome at last struck. Cunobelinus, who alone might have organised a united resistance, was dead; and the Emperor Claudius saw an opportunity to increase his reputation with an easy victory. Four Legions were assembled—the Second, Fourteenth and Twentieth from the Rhineland and the Ninth from the Upper Danube—and a large force of Auxiliaries with many cavalry. The whole army, numbering about 40,000, was better balanced for fighting in Britain than that of Caesar: and by this time the safe harbour of Richborough was well known to Rome.

The invasion sailed from Boulogne under command of Aulus Plautius and landed at Richborough, where it at once fortified a base with a ditch whose traces may still be seen, and at Dover and Lympne. From this point Caesar's plan was followed, to destroy the Belgic power in the south-east. Cunobelinus's two sons fought, and were beaten, separately. Caratacus was routed on the Stour, near the site of Caesar's victory at Bigbury, but escaped to fight again. Togodumnus, however, who made his stand farther back, was killed. The Britons made a valiant effort to defend the line of the Medway, and were only driven off after a fierce two-day battle, but after this serious resistance collapsed. Claudius then put in an appearance to claim the victory his subordinate had already won, and accepted the submission of the eastern Belgae at their new capital near Colchester.

He lost no time in ordering that new towns on the Roman pattern should be built to replace the huddled huts at Colchester and St. Albans, and endowed the latter with the privileges of a Municipium (see p. 29). The Britons were to become Romans before their wounds had healed.

This submission was soon followed by others. Cogidumnus, king of the West Sussex Regnenses, seems to have turned Roman with alacrity: he adopted the conqueror's name Tiberius Claudius, and received the imposing title of "King and Imperial Representative in Britain". Before long he was building a temple in Chichester to Neptune and Minerva, dedicated in an elegant Latin inscription "for the welfare of the Imperial House". In a less spectacular fashion the king of the Iceni also submitted and became a tributary, as did Queen Cartimandua of the Brigantes. But the will to fight was not dead in either of these peoples, and

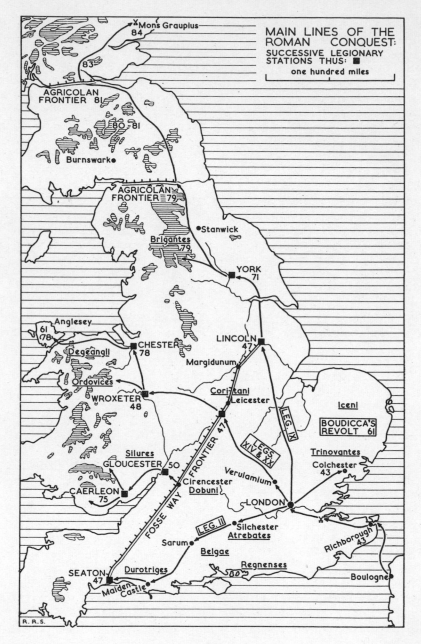

MAIN LINES OF THE
ROMAN CONQUEST:
SUCCESSIVE LEGIONARY
STATIONS THUS: ■

one hundred miles

Mons Graupius
84
83

AGRICOLAN
FRONTIER 81

80-81

Burnswark●

AGRICOLAN
FRONTIER 79

●Stanwick

Brigantes
79

YORK
71

Anglesey

61
(78)

Degeangli

CHESTER
78

LINCOLN
47

Margidunum

Ordovices

Coritani
Leicester

WROXETER
48

LEG. IX

Iceni

BOUDICCA'S
REVOLT 61

Silures

GLOUCESTER 50

LEGS.
XIV & XX

Trinovantes

Colchester
43

CAERLEON
75

Cirencester
Dobuni

Verulamium

LONDON

FOSSE WAY   FRONTIER 47

LEG. II

Silchester
Atrebates

Sarum

Belgae

Regnenses

Richborough
43

SEATON
47

Durotriges

Maiden
Castle

Boulogne

R. R. S.

14

Caratacus had escaped to Wales to organise new resistance.

THE CONQUEST OF THE LOWLANDS

After this sweeping initial success, Aulus Plautius continued the conquest and pacification. From a base at London (where a small trading settlement seems to have grown up already before the invasion) he planned a triple thrust west, north-west, and north. Building roads as they went, the Legionaries methodically advanced across country. The Ninth took the line of the Great North Road towards Lincoln, the Fourteenth and Twentieth that of Watling Street into the Midlands, and the Second the route to Silchester and the west. The first two columns seem to have met little opposition, but the Second Legion under the future Emperor Vespasian had the great hill-forts of the western Belgae to deal with. Vespasian claimed to have fought thirty battles and stormed over twenty forts; and among the latter was certainly Maiden Castle, where excavation has recently revealed the skeletons of defenders buried where they fell. One still has the head of a Roman ballista-bolt embedded in his spine. No trace of siege-works has been found, and the testudo and the Roman artillery were apparently enough to carry even these mighty works by storm.

By A.D. 47, when Aulus Plautius gave up his command to Ostorius Scapula, the Ninth Legion had reached Lincoln, the centre column was deep in the Midlands, and the Second was on the Devon border. Before the advance could go much farther, it was necessary to consolidate what had already been gained; and the first act of Ostorius was to halt the Legions and connect their positions with the Fosse Way as a temporary frontier. From Seaton on the Devon coast, where the Second was temporarily quartered, the road with its earthwork forts for Auxiliaries was laid out in an almost direct line to the station of the Ninth at Lincoln. On its way it passed through the capitals of the Dobuni and Coritani at Cirencester and Leicester, and its garrisons were intended to protect these people, and all others who had submitted, from the still hostile Silures and others without. Within the line the Britons were to be disarmed, and when the Iceni objected they were overpowered. One of the original forts on this line is known, at Margidunum, half-way between Leicester and Lincoln. With its six concentric ditches it was evidently designed to protect an Auxiliary garrison which might be penned in by overwhelming numbers.

In the next year Ostorius felt sufficiently secure in his rear to press the advance farther. The Fourteenth and Twentieth were moved forward, with the Watling Street, to Wroxeter, and operations started against the Degeangli of North Wales. Farther south Caratacus, at the head of the Silures, was giving serious trouble to the isolated forts of the Fosse frontier, and the Second Legion was moved out to Gloucester to check him. Undaunted, Caratacus moved on to the Ordovices of North Wales and continued the struggle until he was once more routed. His last hope lay with the Yorkshire Brigantes, amongst whom there were many eager to fight against Rome. Queen Cartimandua, however, had submitted and allied herself with Rome, and

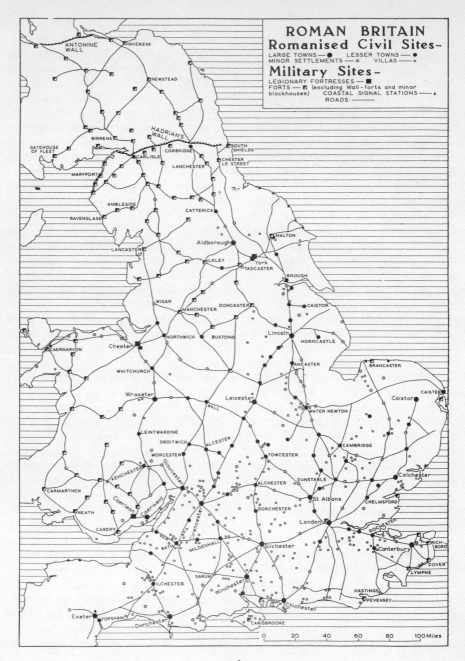

ROMAN BRITAIN
Romanised Civil Sites—
LARGE TOWNS ● LESSER TOWNS ●
MINOR SETTLEMENTS ○ VILLAS —
Military Sites—
LEGIONARY FORTRESSES ■
FORTS — ▣ (excluding Wall-forts and minor blockhouses) COASTAL SIGNAL STATIONS — ▲
ROADS —

ANTONINE WALL
INVERESK
NEWSTEAD
HADRIAN'S WALL
BIRRENS
GATEHOUSE OF FLEET
SOUTH SHIELDS
CARLISLE
CORBRIDGE
CHESTER LE STREET
LANCHESTER
MARYPORT
AMBLESIDE
CATTERICK
RAVENGLASS
MALTON
LANCASTER
Aldborough
ILKLEY
York
TADCASTER
BROUGH
WIGAN
DONCASTER
MANCHESTER
CAISTOR
Lincoln
CAERNARVON
Chester
NORTHWICH
BUXTON
HORNCASTLE
ANCASTER
BRANCASTER
WHITCHURCH
Wroxeter
WALL
Leicester
Caistor
CAISTER
WATER NEWTON
LEINTWARDINE
DROITWICH
ALCESTER
WORCESTER
TOWCESTER
CAMBRIDGE
KENCHESTER
Gloucester
ALCHESTER
DUNSTABLE
Colchester
CARMARTHEN
Cirencester
DORCHESTER
St. Albans
CHELMSFORD
Caerleon
Caerwent
London
NEATH
ROCHESTER
RICH-BORO
CARDIFF
BATH
MILDENHALL
Silchester
Canterbury
DOVER
SARUM
LYMPNE
Winchester
HASTINGS
ILCHESTER
PEVENSEY
Exeter
TOPSHAM
Dorchester
Chichester
CARISBROOKE

| 0   20   40   60   80   100 Miles |

16

relied on Roman aid against her own turbulent subjects. She handed Caratacus over, and he was sent to Rome to grace a Triumph and end his days in captivity.

Some Legionaries were already finishing their time of service, and in accordance with Roman practice Ostorius established a "Colonia" (see p. 29) for retired veterans at Colchester. It was expected that they would help to overawe the doubtful Iceni; but their establishment involved expelling the local British landowners, and gave further cause for resentment.

(see p. 29)

BOUDICCA'S REVOLT

With the arrival of Suetonius Paulinus in A.D. 59 the advance continued into North Wales. With the Legions from Wroxeter he penetrated along the north coast, building forts, and by A.D. 61 reached and crossed the Menai Straits to massacre the Druids who were the implacable enemies of Rome. While he was so engaged, the storm which had long been brewing broke far in his rear.

Claudius had recognised the King of the Iceni as a tributary, but on his death Nero decreed that the kingdom should be directly ruled by Rome. His orders were brutally carried out by his Procurator (see p. 27), who sacked the palace, flogged the king's widow Boudicca, seized as slaves the nobles who resisted, and then demanded recruits and tribute. On top of their previous grievances, this was too much: the Iceni rallied round Boudicca, and were joined by the Trinovantes who had not forgotten the seizure of their lands at Colchester. Weapons hidden during the disarmament, or made surreptitiously since, were produced, and a

(see p. 27)

war of extermination declared against everything Roman. The troops were far away, and the new towns at St. Albans, Colchester, and London were in easy reach and without defences. All three were burned and their inhabitants massacred: a last stand in the new Temple of Claudius at Colchester lasted only two days, and 2,000 Legionaries sent too late from the Ninth at Lincoln were overwhelmed. Suetonius was 200 miles distant, and the temporary commander of the Second Legion at Gloucester was too scared to move. Nothing could be done to save the towns, but when Boudicca's excited hordes crashed into Suetonius and his troops on Watling Street the Britons were utterly routed. Boudicca took poison, and the revolt collapsed as quickly as it had arisen, but the Roman Government had learnt a lesson. When Suetonius started reprisals he was recalled, and a new Governor was sent with orders to avoid any repetition of the treatment which had produced the trouble.

Most of the Lowland zone was now pacified. For some years the frontier halted, and the Fourteenth Legion was finally withdrawn from Britain in A.D. 69. But the conquest was far from complete. Before long the Brigantes drove out their queen and turned openly hostile, and had to be dealt with. In 71 Vespasian, now Emperor, moved the Ninth Legion forward to York and built a fort at Malton to dominate the best cornlands of the tribe. After three years fighting, including the destruction of their huge but unfinished fortress at Stanwick, their power (but not their spirit) was broken. On the Welsh border the Second Legion moved up to its new quarters at Caerleon in

A bird's-eye view of Roman Caerwent, tribal capital of the Silures.

75, and the Silures were finally de-
feated and induced to begin a new
Romanised capital at Caerwent. From
Caerleon, roads and forts began to
stretch out into the south and centre of
Wales to hold down the hills.

AGRICOLA

With the appointment of Agricola as
Governor in 78 came the last and
most impressive stage of the Conquest.
After moving the Twentieth to Chester,
and reconquering North Wales and
Anglesey, Agricola turned his attention
to the north. In 79 he overran the
Pennine homeland of the Brigantes and
set garrisons to hold them down, and ran
a line of earthwork forts across the island
from Tyne to Solway. With his rear
secured, his main advance into Scotland
began in the following year. Here there
were hill-forts so strong or inaccessible
that one at least, at Burnswark in Dum-
friesshire, compelled him to conduct a
regular siege. But the advance went on
with the methodical remorselessness of
Rome, studding the country with forts as
it proceeded.

By 81 he had reached the Forth–
Clyde line, and built another line of
barrier-forts. For a year he then halted to
prepare an invasion of Ireland, but never
carried it out: the gathering of Picts in
the Highlands probably made it too
dangerous. In 83 he pressed farther
north, by way of Stirling and the east
coast, keeping touch with his fleet, and
in A.D. 84 routed the Picts in a great battle
at some spot called "Mons Graupius".
His intention was to conquer the whole
island, but his recall in 85 prevented
him carrying it out. Historians still differ

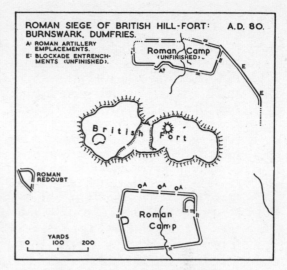

*The Roman siege-works comprise a com-
pleted camp covering the main water-
supply of the British fort, an unfinished
camp to the north, and unfinished blockade
entrenchments. The fort evidently fell before
the later works were completed.*

as to whether, if he had done so, the Highlands could have been permanently held;
but if they could have been, Britain would
have needed no great defensive barrier
between England and Scotland, and the
addition of Ireland to the Empire might
well have followed.

In 86 a fourth Legion which had
been in Britain since 71 was recalled,
and the number finally reduced to three.
This left no spare Legion to station in the
Scottish Lowlands, and made farther advance unlikely. For a time some of
Agricola's forts in Scotland were held;
but once the idea of conquering Scotland
had been given up they were mostly too
remote to be worth retaining.

THE CONSOLIDATION OF THE
FRONTIER

After the reign of Trajan the Roman Empire practically ceased to expand. It had reached the natural frontiers of the Rhine, the Danube, the mountains of Asia Minor, and the Arabian and Sahara Deserts, and the emphasis changed to the consolidation of these frontiers for permanent defence. Britain was no exception. Once the project of conquering the whole island had been dropped, the two possible lines for a frontier were those with the shortest distance from sea to sea: namely from Forth to Clyde and from Tyne to Solway. The former, though much shorter, was far distant from the Legionary bases at York and Chester, and its occupation in strength would also have involved the permanent garrisoning of much untamed hill-country in its rear. The Tyne–Solway line was therefore adopted as the permanent frontier, though outpost forts beyond it continued to be held.

Trajan began the reorganisation by fortifying the Stanegate road (built by Agricola) between Carlisle and the Tyne at Corbridge, and by a general rebuilding of forts in stone instead of earthwork and timber. The three Legionary fortresses were reconstructed in masonry early in the second century, as were many Auxiliary forts. The garrison too was regrouped: some of Agricola's forts in the far north were abandoned and their Cohorts moved to the new frontier, and some troops in Wales and northern England were moved to new sites. At Castleshaw, above Manchester, a large fort was replaced by a small police blockhouse, while an entirely new fort was built at Hardknot Pass in Cumberland. The general picture is of concentration towards the new line.

Early in the reign of Hadrian (117–138) there seems to have been trouble in Britain. In circumstances at which we can only guess, the Ninth Legion disappeared. Probably the Brigantes were at it again, and that unlucky force had been so cut up as to be disbanded. Hadrian was an indefatigable traveller, visiting and supervising province after province, and it was not long before he appeared to put things right. In 122, he arrived and personally inspected the defences. By this year we find a new Legion, the Sixth, at York, and it is probable that Hadrian brought it with him to replace the Ninth.

HADRIAN'S WALL

The result of his visit was the magnificent work known ever since as Hadrian's Wall. Sited some distance north of the Stanegate, along ridges forming a better tactical position, it extended from Wallsend on the Tyne to Bowness far down the Solway Estuary. Between the River Irthing and Bowness it was originally made of clay or turf, and only gradually rebuilt in stone, but in its final form it was a wall of stone and concrete eight or ten feet wide, perhaps twenty feet high with its parapet, and 73 miles long. At intervals along its line were sixteen forts for Cohorts of 500 or 1,000 Auxiliaries. A fort at South Shields covered the south bank of the Tyne below Wallsend, and a line of forts and signal stations stretched down the Cumberland coast. The front was covered by a ditch 30 feet wide and 9 feet deep (except where the slope made this

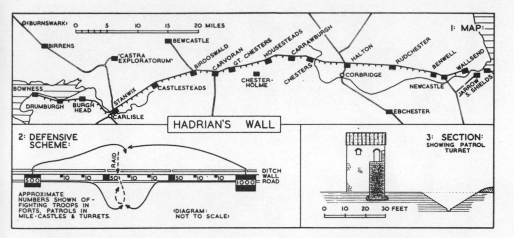

unnecessary) and the gaps between the forts were protected by "milecastles" at mile intervals. Each milecastle housed a patrol responsible for its own length of rampart, and two signal towers stood at equal intervals between each pair of mile-castles.

Gates through the wall, and steps to its rampart walk, occurred only in the forts and milecastles. It was not built to withstand a serious attack at any point of its line, for few men could be massed on top of it and it would have been difficult even with the ladders in the towers to re-inforce them. The purpose was to deter raiding parties and prevent infiltration between the forts until the garrisons could be warned and led out to beat off the attack in the open. For this it was better to have few stairways, and to cover them all with a defensible building.

Some 2 million cubic yards of earth and rock had to be moved to make the ditch, and about the same amount of stone and concrete went into the construction of the wall. Legionaries built it, "centuries" of

eighty to ninety men being responsible for small sections of about forty yards and signing their work with a simple inscription. With the exception of some temporary drafts from the Second Legion, however, its garrison was Auxiliary: about 10,000 field troops in the forts, and a patrolling force in the milecastles whose job was to give the alarm and hold on as best they could until help arrived. The outposts north of the wall, and the forts and signal stations of the Cumberland coast and Tyne mouth, may have brought the total up to nearly 20,000 men.

THE VALLUM

South of the wall, for most of its length, runs an earthwork which is still something of a puzzle. This, known nowa-days as the "Vallum", is a flat-bottomed ditch with its earth thrown up into equal mounds revetted with turfwork on either side. It is now known to have been made at the same time as the wall, and the only crossings left by the diggers were op-posite the fort gateways (where both

A Milecastle on Hadrian's Wall.

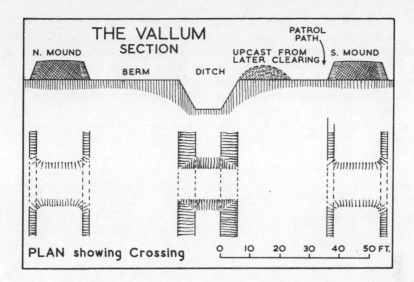

THE VALLUM
SECTION

N. MOUND   BERM   DITCH   PATROL PATH   S. MOUND

UPCAST FROM LATER CLEARING

PLAN showing Crossing   0 10 20 30 40 50 FT.

mounds are broken) and at milecastles (where the north mound is broken but the south is not). It cannot, from its design, have been a defence work, but it would certainly have obstructed movement from either side. Crossings at forts were clearly intended for through traffic, but those at milecastles were not: it seems the milecastle garrisons used it as a ground-level patrol track, which would allow them to deal with smugglers or intruders who could not be reached from the top of the wall.

Its construction would have required a year's labour by 3,000 men, and to justify this it must have served some important purpose. One suggestion is that it marked the customs boundary for the officials of the civil Procurator, whose department was quite separate from that of the Army, and that it avoided putting civil officials into the gateways of military forts. If so, this cannot long have been the practice, for soon after its construction it was obliterated in the neighbourhood of the forts and for most of its length its mounds were breached and causeways thrown across it at intervals of some forty-five yards. It must have been a nuisance to fort garrisons, and it is possible that the customs boundary was temporarily moved when the Antonine Wall was built.

This was not the end of its career, however, for at a later date—perhaps after the northern wall was abandoned—these crossings were demolished, and still later the ditch was cleared out again except near the forts. Its function as a civil boundary and an obstacle to illegal traffic seems to have continued.

In Hadrian's time the Army in Britain seems to have included 38,000 Auxiliaries (of which over a fifth were cavalry) in addition to the three Legions. When the wall and the other forts in the north had been provided for, only some twenty

23

Auxiliary cohorts were left for all the rest of the Province, and some more Welsh and Pennine forts had to be evacuated. About this time there is a sudden growth of native hill-fort towns in Wales, and it is likely that with the removal of most of the garrison the tribesmen were encouraged, or at least allowed, to provide for their own defence. That the Welsh at this time were no danger to the Lowlands is shown by the fact that the Second Legion at Caerleon was consistently kept under strength, with drafts absent for long periods in the north.

THE ANTONINE WALL

Hadrian's Wall was completed, apart from the rebuilding of the turf section, about 127, and so long as Hadrian lived it remained the frontier. Soon after the accession of Antoninus Pius, however, we find an ambitious scheme for throwing forward the defences for which the reasons are by no means clear. In 140 the Governor Lollius Urbicus advanced up Agricola's grass-grown road into Scotland, and two years later a second barrier-wall was constructed between Forth and Clyde. This Antonine Wall was a much simplified version of Hadrian's work. It had no Vallum, and no patrol posts between the forts, and was built of turf or clay on a stone foundation, 14 feet wide at the base and perhaps 12 feet high with a palisade. Its ditch, however, was larger, averaging 40 feet wide by 12 feet deep; and its earthwork forts, though very small, were much closer together—nineteen in 37 miles of wall.

The work was planned to economise garrison as well as labour, for the Army of Britain was seriously strained by this new commitment. Sometimes one Cohort sufficed to man two forts, and the total force cannot have been much more than 6,000. All three Legions sent drafts to the new wall, showing that it could only be held by weakening the field army. Meanwhile, though the forts on Hadrian's Wall were still occupied, the southern wall itself was temporarily abandoned: its patrolling garrison was withdrawn, and its milecastle gates dismantled. It was probably at this time that the Vallum was breached with crossings.

The most likely explanation of this curious move is that it was designed to cut off the tribes of southern Scotland, which were becoming increasingly dangerous, and to make possible the depopulation of the area by the well-known Roman practice of deporting peoples *en masse*. Evidence that considerable numbers were shifted from Britain to the Rhineland at this time may bear this out. The whole scheme may only have been intended as temporary, and such it certainly proved. The Army was too thinly spread: garrisons in Wales and the Pennines were cut to danger level, and in 154 the Brigantes broke into revolt. They were suppressed in the following year, and a new fort built at Brough to control them, but the position was clearly dangerous. After this, and the first collapse of the Antonine line, the gates and patrols of Hadrian's Wall were replaced.

The Antonine Wall relied on Roman ships to protect its flanks on the estuaries of Forth and Clyde, and on the Clyde this failed. A harbour beyond the wall at Dumbarton had to be abandoned, and it seems that Irish pirates were already making the seas on that side unsafe. Without

24

this security the wall could easily be out-flanked, and must soon become untenable. Twice, about 158 and 182, it was wrecked. It was again re-occupied for a short time, but in or soon after 185 its garrisons buried their altars and finally marched south.

SEVERUS REBUILDS HADRIAN'S WALL

Henceforward for two centuries Hadrian's Wall was the frontier, and it was perfectly capable of serving its purpose so long as it was properly manned. But no defensive system is any use without men to hold it, and in 196 the Governor Clodius Albinus marched off the troops to Gaul to make a bid for the Empire. The Picts then swarmed over the wall unopposed and did their best to destroy it. There was no one to interfere, and they methodically wrecked its forts and towers and levelled whole stretches to the ground. The Legionary fortress at York suffered likewise, but there is no

evidence of destruction farther south in the civilian Lowlands. The immense trouble they took to destroy the wall is a testimonial to its importance.

The Emperor Severus, having defeated Albinus, sent back the Army and ordered the immediate repair of the damage. From 197 to 208 rebuilding went on, with the enforced help of the tribal communities of the Lowlands, and when the defences were re-established he came in person to punish the Picts. From 208 for four years he fought his way up the East of Scotland, perhaps as far as Aberdeen, covering Agricola's old ground. His object was terror, not conquest, and when he died at York in 211 the Picts were sufficiently cowed to give no more serious trouble for a hundred years.

FORTS AND MILITARY LIFE

The standard fort of the second century, for an Auxiliary cohort, is illustrated at Ambleside (below). The extreme simplicity of the rampart, with no

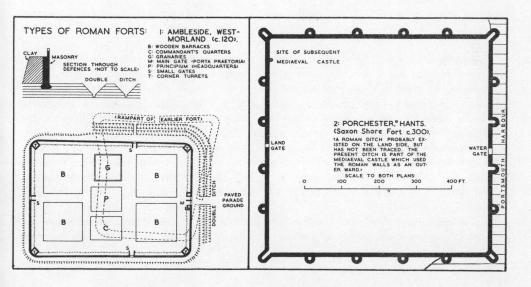

TYPES OF ROMAN FORTS: I: AMBLESIDE, WESTMORLAND (c. 120).

CLAY   MASONRY

SECTION THROUGH DEFENCES (NOT TO SCALE)

DOUBLE DITCH

B: WOODEN BARRACKS
C: COMMANDANT'S QUARTERS
G: GRANARIES
M: MAIN GATE (PORTA PRAETORIA)
P: PRINCIPIUM (HEADQUARTERS)
S: SMALL GATES
T: CORNER TURRETS

(RAMPART OF EARLIER FORT)

DOUBLE DITCH

PAVED PARADE GROUND

SITE OF SUBSEQUENT MEDIAEVAL CASTLE

2: PORCHESTER, HANTS. (Saxon Shore Fort c. 300).
(A ROMAN DITCH PROBABLY EXISTED ON THE LAND SIDE, BUT HAS NOT BEEN TRACED. THE PRESENT DITCH IS PART OF THE MEDIAEVAL CASTLE WHICH USED THE ROMAN WALLS AS AN OUTER WARD.)

LAND GATE

WATER GATE

SCALE TO BOTH PLANS:
0   100   200   300   400 FT.

PORTSMOUTH HARBOUR

LEGIONARY AMPHITHEATRE
CAERLEON

SECTIONAL ELEVATION ON CENTRAL AXIS (RECONSTRUCTED)

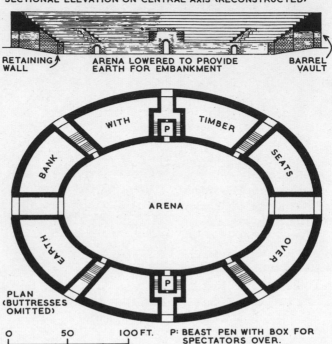

RETAINING WALL

ARENA LOWERED TO PROVIDE EARTH FOR EMBANKMENT

BARREL VAULT

BANK WITH TIMBER SEATS OVER EARTH

ARENA

PLAN (BUTTRESSES OMITTED)

0   50   100 FT.

P: BEAST PEN WITH BOX FOR SPECTATORS OVER.

projecting towers for flanking fire and with wide gateways, shows that it was not intended for prolonged defence against a siege. Its purpose was to protect the troops' quarters and stores from night raids and surprises, and once roused the garrison expected to get through its gates as quickly as possible and fight in the open. Rome was still strong and confident, and did not yet need to use masonry to eke out lack of men.

The oblong shape allowed the interior to be divided by roads into three sections, the centre of which contained the headquarters building (Principia) with the standards and pay-chest, the commandant's house, and the carefully designed granaries for storing corn. In a larger fort it might also hold a hospital and other buildings. The other two sections, each subdivided by a road leading to a gate, held the barracks. In some forts these were built or rebuilt in stone, but at Ambleside they remained (unlike the central block) in timber. They were long narrow buildings of a plan not unlike

26

military hutments of modern times, and no doubt quite as dreary.

Outside the fort and its ditch was a parade ground, often paved, for drill and inspections, and a bath-house. Before long, also, there would be a small huddle of booths and wine-shops ready to provide the soldier with a chance to spend his pay, and an increasing number of "married quarters" as the garrison took local wives. This civil settlement might itself be worth protecting with a rampart as an annexe to the fort.

Garrison life was no doubt then as always nine-tenths boredom, with eternal drill, cleaning of arms and equipment, and aimless off-duty periods. Active duties, unless some large campaign were in progress, would be a matter of patrols and police work. Auxiliary forts did not often have amphitheatres, but doubtless some equivalent of the modern regimental boxing contest was organised by the centurions. The Roman Army, like the Japanese, was largely vegetarian in practice if not in principle: corn was the staple diet, baked into bread or flat bannocks. Imported wine may have been expensive for the rank and file, but British beer and mead filled the gap. It was a rough life; and though the border troops impressed the hill tribesmen with the power of Rome, they could hardly teach them much of the civilisation of which they themselves saw so little.

Auxiliaries often found themselves in bleak and uninviting places, in the uplands of Wales and the north, but the Legionaries were more fortunate. Their fortresses were in the plains, and were more spacious and less remote from civilised life. The Legionary, with his Roman Citizenship and his higher military pay and status, was a cut above his humbler Auxiliary comrade. He mostly escaped the dull and dirty work of everyday frontier patrolling; but he was the real striking force in serious fighting, and his training and discipline were even more rigorous. Building as well as fighting was his job, and he had to be as handy with the trowel as with the sword. Each Legion had a history longer than that of the oldest British regiments, and its Eagle was the centre of a loyalty and tradition passed on for generations.

GOVERNMENT AND ADMINISTRATION

As a province directly under the Emperor's control (as distinct from those in which the Senate had considerable influence) Britain was governed by a "Propraetor". This official corresponded in some ways to the modern Colonial Governor, and served generally for about five years. He was commander-in-chief of the troops, and with one important exception he had the final responsibility for civil government as well. The exception was the "Procurator", head of the revenue department. Though of lower rank than the Propraetor, he was to some extent independent of him—an arrangement intended to prevent Governors enriching themselves at the Emperor's expense.

The benefits of government had as always to be paid for, and the Procurator's men collected from the provincials a personal tax and an assessed tax on land. In addition there were customs duties, such as those collected on Hadrian's Wall, and a burdensome corn levy for feeding the troops. Something was apt to stick to the collector's fingers, and a corn measure

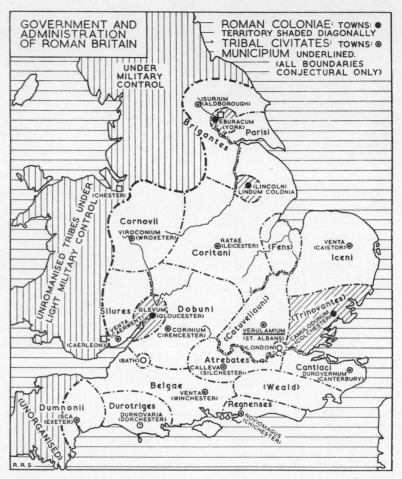

GOVERNMENT AND ADMINISTRATION OF ROMAN BRITAIN

ROMAN COLONIAE: TOWNS: ●
TERRITORY SHADED DIAGONALLY
TRIBAL CIVITATES: TOWNS: ◎
MUNICIPIUM UNDERLINED.
(ALL BOUNDARIES CONJECTURAL ONLY)

UNDER MILITARY CONTROL

ISURIUM (ALDBOROUGH)
EBURACUM (YORK)
Brigantes
Parisi

UNROMANISED TRIBES UNDER LIGHT MILITARY CONTROL

(CHESTER)

(LINCOLN) LINDUM COLONIA

Cornovii
VIROCONIUM (WROXETER)

RATAE (LEICESTER)
Coritani
(Fens)
VENTA (CAISTOR)
Iceni

Silures
GLEVUM
Dobuni (GLOUCESTER)

VENTA (CAERWENT)
(CAERLEON)

CORINIUM (CIRENCESTER)

(Catuvellauni)
VERULAMIUM (ST. ALBANS)
(LONDON)

(Trinovantes)
CAMULODUNUM (COLCHESTER)

(BATH)

Atrebates
CALLEVA (SILCHESTER)

Cantiaci
DUROVERNUM (CANTERBURY)

Belgae
VENTA (WINCHESTER)

(Weald)

(UNORGANISED)

Dumnonii
ISCA (EXETER)

Durotriges
DURNOVARIA (DORCHESTER)

Regnenses

NOVIOMAGUS (CHICHESTER)

R.R.S.

has been found which is stamped as containing only seven-eighths of what it really holds—the odd eighth being no doubt an official perquisite. Besides general revenue, the Procurator managed the large Imperial Estates and mining monopoly, and British lead was an important source of government income.

LOCAL GOVERNMENT

The backward areas of the Highland zone were no doubt under direct military control, or, like Cornwall, left to their own devices as long as they gave no trouble. But in the Lowlands it was the wise practice of Rome to encourage the civilised tribes to manage their own local affairs. Their leading men were easily persuaded to adopt a Roman way of life, and from the start the Government encouraged them to build new capitals of

28

Roman type. The tribal nobles became the "Senate", and little more than a change of names was needed to produce a local government on the Roman pattern. Most of the Lowlands could thus be divided into tribal units called "Civitates", with county towns in which the chief men and magistrates met to raise rates and transact business. There were over a dozen such towns, but as far as we know only one (Verulamium) was actually given the privileges of a Municipium (a chartered native community, with some independence of Government officials).

Besides these there were towns of direct Roman foundation known as Coloniae, which, at least in origin, were settlements of retired Legionaries who were Roman Citizens. Colchester, Lincoln, Gloucester, and the town which grew up alongside the Legionary fortress at York were of this type. They had a charter similar to that of the Municipium, with magistrates called Decuriones elected by the citizens, and a Senate of ex-magistrates. Their inhabitants had farmlands outside the town, and a considerable area was "attributed" to each Colonia for purposes of courts and police and the raising of rates for public buildings and services.

Small towns, of which there were many in Britain, also had some measure of control over local affairs. Civil settlements outside forts, small market-towns, and posting-stations on main roads, might be recognised as "Vici" and allowed to raise and spend a public fund, though they had no "attributed" territory.

But in the Roman Empire "representative government" did not reach beyond local affairs. There was indeed a Provincial Council, representing the various communities, which met at first at Colchester and later probably at London; but its chief business was to choose a High Priest to organise the official Emperor Worship in the Province, and to raise funds for the purpose. Cases are known where such a Council protested to the Emperor against an unpopular Governor, but of the doings of the British Council we have no record.

THE CAPITAL

London was exceptional among Romano-British towns. It was far the largest, and the most flourishing, yet we have no knowledge of its receiving chartered rank. It was not a tribal capital, yet it was the centre of the road system and of industry and trade. As a commercial place it probably had and needed no "attributed" territory, and therefore played no part in local government outside its walls: but it seems the obvious site for the capital of the Province. The Procurator certainly had his headquarters there, and it is very likely that after a time the Governor did likewise. A fort was built and garrisoned here by the end of the first century, which was normal in provincial capitals but otherwise unknown in civil towns. Military headquarters, however, was probably at York.

Until the time of Severus, Britain was a single Province; but the exploits of Albinus seem to have shown the desirability of dividing the command of its forces. Severus cut it in two. We do not know his boundary, but from the fact that York and Lincoln were in "Lower Britain" and Chester and Caerleon in

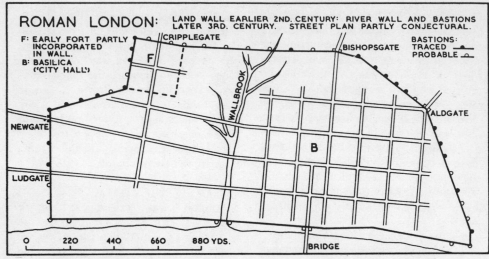

ROMAN LONDON: LAND WALL EARLIER 2ND. CENTURY: RIVER WALL AND BASTIONS LATER 3RD. CENTURY. STREET PLAN PARTLY CONJECTURAL.

F: EARLY FORT PARTLY INCORPORATED IN WALL.
B: BASILICA ("CITY HALL")

CRIPPLEGATE
BISHOPSGATE
BASTIONS:
TRACED
PROBABLE
WALLBROOK
ALDGATE
NEWGATE
B
LUDGATE
BRIDGE

0   220   440   660   880 YDS.

The main built-up area lay to the east of the Wallbrook, round the Basilica and bridgehead. The wall was built to connect with the N.E. and S.W. angles of an earlier fort which may originally have protected the military depot and supplies after their destruction by Boudicca. The bridge over the Thames was of timber-pile construction, and there was a small suburb around its southern end, at Southwark.

"Upper", it may have run from the Mersey to the Wash. This arrangement would divide the Army about equally between two Governors—two Legions and the Auxiliaries in the remaining Welsh forts to one, and one Legion and the bulk of the Auxiliary forces to the other. In such an arrangement, London and York would almost certainly be the two capitals.

ROMANISATION OF THE LOWLANDS:
TOWNS

Of the million or so inhabitants of Roman Britain, the Occupation may have accounted for perhaps 100,000. About half this number were soldiers, and the rest officials, merchants, craftsmen, and the assorted hangers-on who follow in the wake of armies. Most of the troops, and probably the majority also of the others, came from near-by parts of the Empire whose peoples were not very different from the Britons; and there seems to have been no noticeable effect on the physical type of the population.

Behind the screen of the frontier armies, and with the organisation of civil government, the process of Romanisation soon got under way. Its chief centres, at least in the first two centuries, were the new towns, embodying that idea of the city as a centre of civilised life which was new to Britain but old in the Mediterranean lands. Previous tribal capitals had been overgrown villages, with none of

30

the amenities that Rome considered essential, and the Britons had therefore to be taught, aided, and encouraged to build themselves towns of Roman style. Starting from scratch, or in some cases with existing hut-capitals, they concentrated first on public buildings and then rebuilt their houses and surrounded the whole with walls.

Agricola was the first Governor to make a special effort to encourage town development, and from his time onwards for half a century or more the towns of Roman Britain were taking the shape which they were to keep, more or less, for the rest of the Occupation. The tribal Senates were helped with money where necessary, and with the loan of Legionary engineers and surveyors, to plan rectangular street layouts, to build a forum, basilica, baths, and walls, and to lay on a water-supply. At the same time they gradually learnt Latin, copied Roman manners of dress and furniture, and adapted themselves to their new position as members of the Empire.

The time of town construction in Britain was also that of Rome's greatest power and confidence, and the plans show an optimism which later events were to belie. Though very small to modern eyes, the towns were laid out with plenty of room for future increase of population. The walls enclosed much empty ground, and Silchester, with one hundred acres, had only eighty houses. The Basilica or town hall could seat the entire population comfortably, as could the Amphitheatre erected outside the walls, and the baths were large enough to take hundreds of people at once. Gateways were built as monuments of civic pride rather than as

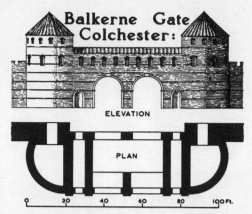

ELEVATION

PLAN

0   20   40   60   80   100 Ft.

Built in the first century, with the town walls, probably soon after the destruction of the place by Boudicca. Its curious plan, projecting from the wall instead of being flanked by protecting towers, and the size of its openings, show that it was built for display rather than as a serious fortification.

fortifications, and even tiny places boasted an imposing town wall.

Sometimes, even at this period, optimism outran performance, and the Cornovii of Wroxeter started a bath-house which they never finished. Most of the towns of Roman Britain were artificial creations rather than natural developments, and this was to become increasingly obvious as the years went by.

TOWN LIFE AND BUILDINGS

As completed, the normal type of "large" town (by which we mean a tribal capital of anything from 40 to 240 acres) centred on its Basilica and Forum. The Basilica, on which the earliest Christian churches were modelled, had aisles and a central nave, with a double row of pillars supporting a clerestory. Here the tribal

31

BASILICA AND FORUM: SILCHESTER.

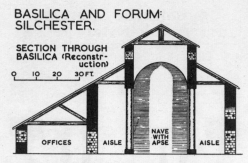

SECTION THROUGH BASILICA (Reconstruction)

0   10   20   30 FT.

OFFICES   AISLE   NAVE WITH APSE   AISLE

PLAN OF BASILICA AND FORUM:

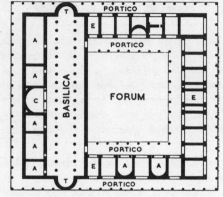

PORTICO

PORTICO

BASILICA   FORUM

PORTICO

PORTICO

A: ADMINISTRATIVE OFFICES.   C: CURIA (COUNCIL CHAMBER)
E: ENTRANCE.   T: TRIBUNE (MAGISTRATE'S OFFICIAL SEAT).
OTHER COMPARTMENTS MOSTLY SHOPS.
0   50   100   150   200   250   300 FEET

Senate met, local business was dealt with, and justice dispensed. This lay on one side of the Forum, which was a market square surrounded by shops on the other three sides.

Around the Forum the town was laid out in rectangular blocks, with straight streets, and the ordinary house in the busy parts was a long barn-like building with its front end sometimes open to the road as a shop. Here, as in the Middle Ages, the craftsman could be seen making the goods which he exposed for sale. Though it had a stone foundation, it was generally constructed with a timber frame and plaster panels similar to those of late medieval and Tudor times.

The Baths, which were a place for meeting friends and spending leisure as much as a means to cleanliness, were of the type we now call "Turkish". All normally had at least three rooms of different temperatures—the frigidarium with a cold plunge, the tepidarium, which was warm, and the caldarium, which was hot enough to produce perspiration and contained hot water. Some also had a sudatorium or sweat-room where the temperature was particularly fierce, and

PLAN OF THE PUBLIC BATHS AT SILCHESTER SLIGHTLY SIMPLIFIED

ORIGINAL PLAN BLOCKED IN: LATER EXTENSIONS SHADED.

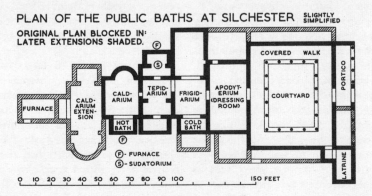

FURNACE   CALD-ARIUM EXTEN-SION   CALD-ARIUM   TEPID-ARIUM   FRIGID-ARIUM   APODYT-ERIUM (DRESSING ROOM)   COVERED WALK   PORTICO
HOT BATH   COLD BATH   COURTYARD
(F) - FURNACE
(S) - SUDATORIUM   LATRINE

0 10 20 30 40 50 60 70 80 90 100   150 FEET

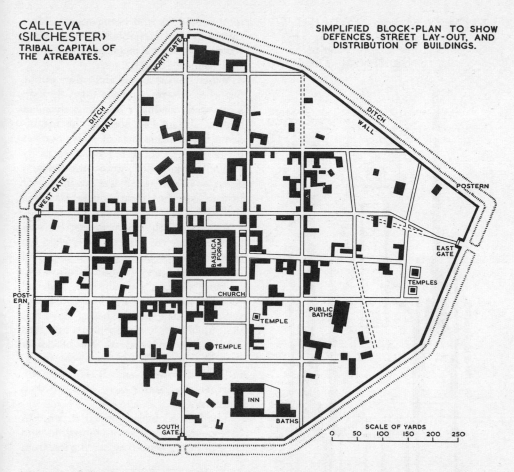

CALLEVA
(SILCHESTER)
TRIBAL CAPITAL OF
THE ATREBATES.

SIMPLIFIED BLOCK-PLAN TO SHOW
DEFENCES, STREET LAY-OUT, AND
DISTRIBUTION OF BUILDINGS.

Plan of Silchester: The original defences were a ditch and earth rampart, laid out early in the Roman period, and the wall was later built (probably in the early second century) on the narrow berm between rampart and ditch. This left no room for projecting towers, and the gates were therefore recessed. The main street, along which passed all traffic between London and the west, ran between the East and West Gates; and most of the shop-fronted strip-houses of craftsmen and tradesmen lay alongside this between the Forum and West Gate. These houses are clearly distinguishable on the plan from the large court-yard-dwellings of the wealthy. An amphitheatre lay a short distance outside the eastern angle of the wall.

33

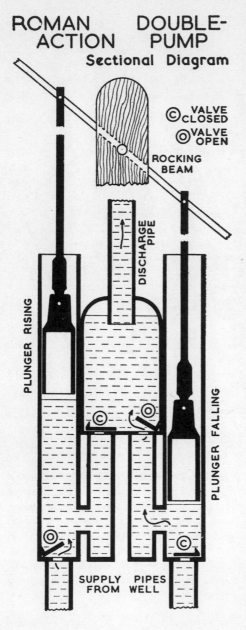

ROMAN DOUBLE-ACTION PUMP
Sectional Diagram

© VALVE CLOSED
Ⓞ VALVE OPEN

ROCKING BEAM

DISCHARGE PIPE

PLUNGER RISING

PLUNGER FALLING

SUPPLY FROM WELL

PIPES

most would have dressing-rooms. Heat from a furnace passed beneath the floors, warmed water in a metal cauldron in the caldarium and heated the air.

Water for the Baths and other public purposes was run into the town through a covered conduit from a convenient stream. Britain had none of the magnificent bridge-aqueducts of Italy, but her towns were so small and water so easily available that they were unnecessary. Surplus public water was available for private use, but most houses also had their wells.

Away from the main streets, set well back in plenty of garden space, were the town houses of the tribal rich men and landowners. These were built round two or more sides of a quadrangle, and had enough rooms for a large household with servants. They had no baths, however; the public bath-house open to all citizens made these unnecessary. No blocks of flats, like those in Rome, have been traced in British towns, and it is uncertain whether any houses were of more than one storey.

The four Coloniae tended in time to become mainly British in population, and little different, with their territories, from

---

The principle of this pump (an example of which was found at Silchester) was invented by Ctesibus of Alexandria in the late second century B.C. Its working depends on flap-valves which open and shut automatically under suction or pressure, and it provides a constant discharge of water. The same principle was still used in fire-engines of the late seventeenth to early nineteenth centuries.

tribal capitals. Two places, however, kept a distinct character of their own: London, with its area of half a square mile and its mixed trading population, and Bath, where the famous medicinal waters attracted the wealthy and gouty in the second century as in the eighteenth. Perhaps a third may be added in the small Roman spa at Buxton, frequented by the officers of the northern garrisons.

Within these towns was to be found the most "Romanised" life in Britain, and it was open to all classes of the free population. Here before long even workmen knew Latin, and goods and craft-products of Roman type were made and used. The amenities of town life as the Romans understood it—the Baths, the amusements of the Amphitheatre, the Forum, the benefits of paved streets and policed town walls—were open to the town-dweller. But townsmen were a small and privileged class—perhaps one in twenty of the population—and the upkeep of public works and services had to be paid for by levies on the dependent territory in general. The towns of Roman Britain were a luxury for which the countryman paid, and their service as craft- and market-centres hardly justified their expense. Apart from their inhabitants, the only gainer was the Imperial Government for which they greatly simplified the business of local administration.

In addition to the more important places, some fifty settlements are classed as "small towns" because they were Romanised and not farming communities, though in size they were little more than villages. Such were the "Vici" mentioned previously. They were often walled, but their public buildings were on a much less lavish scale and they had no considerable area from which they could draw rates for their support, nor would they be much frequented by the tribal nobility. If tribal capitals are considered as "county towns", these would be minor "urban districts".

VILLAS

Next to the towns, the chief centres of Romanised life in Britain were the Villas. These were farm-houses, standing isolated in their own land, and built in Roman fashion. The earliest or poorest were very simple structures like miniature basilicas, with rooms formed by partitions between the upright beams. Most of the five hundred or so which have been discovered, however, had a range of rooms opening on to a corridor or courtyard, and were timber-framed on stone foundations, with roofs of tile or slate. Nearly all had some rooms heated by hypocausts (hot air carried from a furnace under floors raised on pillars) and most had baths. Floors of tesserae or small brick

SMALL VILLA DWELLING-HOUSE
'WINGED CORRIDOR' TYPE

35

A Romano-British Villa

1 Main Entrance 2 Courtyard 3 Outer Ctyd.
4 Business Yard 5 Private Ctyd. serving living
quarters 6 Slaves quarters 7 Workshops 8 Well
9 Hot, Tepid & Cold Bath 10 Drawing Room 11 Stokehole
& Furnace 12 Rooms heated by hypocausts or wall Flues
13 Great Barn 14 Threshing Floor 15 Stables & cow houses

tiles were common, the best rooms sometimes having mosaic, and wall-plaster was generally painted. Articles found in them show that the standard of living, at least in good times, was high, and that pottery and metalware of Roman type were in everyday use.

Nine-tenths of the known Villas lie south-east of a line from Severn to Trent, and most of them are on sheltered sites on southern or eastern slopes, protected from wind and open to the sun. Unlike unromanised farms, they are rarely found on hill-tops; and generally they are close to running water.

The map of Roman Britain produced by the Ordnance Survey shows that Villas tend to cluster in areas favoured by soil and climate, while other districts such as Salisbury Plain and Cranborne Chase, which were thickly populated, have hardly any. One explanation may be that the area of the Western Belgae, who put up a vigorous resistance to the Conquest, became Imperial Domain, and their population continued to be taxed too heavily to "modernize" their farms or methods. Elsewhere, it was only the wealthier landowners who could afford a Roman-style building, and who had the capital to cultivate larger fields and deeper soils with a heavy plough, so producing a market surplus which kept them prosperous. The origins of Villa agriculture may lie in the larger pre-Conquest Belgic farms, some of which certainly had their buildings later on rebuilt in Roman style: but new ones continued to be founded well into the fourth century, and men who were wealthy enough to build on this scale could also afford a good site and good soil. Nearly all Villa-owners were British

tribal gentry, though occasionally some official or merchant from the Continent may have lived in one.

Villas, unlike towns, grew naturally and needed no artificial encouragement. Wealthy Britons, then as now, liked the life of a country gentleman, and simply added to it some Roman comfort and elegance. The labouring staff also lived on or about the place; and though they did not enjoy hypocausts and similar refinements, their quarters were at least better than native huts.

In the fourth century, when sheep farming and cloth production became profitable, a number of Villas cut down their labour force, turned over much of their land to sheep, and installed fulling machinery or other cloth-apparatus on the premises. But they remained firmly based on the land, able to supply most of their own wants, and much less liable to disaster in difficult times than the artificially established town. Consequently, as we shall see, they continued to flourish long after the towns had begun to decay.

NATIVE FARMSTEADS

The majority of Britons continued, throughout the Roman Occupation, to live in hamlets or farmsteads like those of pre-Roman times. The circular huts clustered with no sign of Roman orderliness, and agriculture in the neighbouring plots showed no signs of improvement. Coins and pottery show that some had a surplus to sell and could buy Roman products, and a few made interesting efforts to copy the domestic comforts of the Villas. One such at Woodcutts in Dorset had painted plaster on some hut walls, though the structures once thought to be crude hypocausts now prove to belong to corn-drying kilns and not to living quarters. There was even a tiny amphitheatre. This settlement had existed before the Conquest, and was only gradually affected by Roman contacts. Its ninety-five huts (only a few of which would be standing at any one time) were completely native in plan, and so was the rampart.

Woodcutts was deep in the civilised area, and not far from the Roman road between Old Sarum and Dorchester. Settlements more remote from such centres show much less Roman influence, and in the Highland zone they generally reveal none at all. Contact with civilisation was not in the long run an unmixed blessing, for throughout the Empire the lot of the peasants became increasingly hard in the third and fourth centuries as landowners became more grasping and the Government demanded higher taxes. In Gaul there were frequent peasant revolts, and it is likely that there was similar trouble in Britain. The native farmsteads had no means of quickly expanding production to meet heavier demands, and there are signs that their population fell rather than rose during the later Roman period. The increasing wool-production which brought prosperity to the Villas accompanied the desertion of unromanised farms, and peasants may actually have been turned out to make way for sheep (as happened in Tudor times). Woodcutts was abandoned in the fourth century after a period of decline, and it was by no means exceptional. Skeletons of people who had died by violence were found on the site and they may have perished at the hands of Roman troops. There is also evidence in some places for the deliberate killing of infants, which was a sign of despair not infrequent in late Roman times.

But while the peasant settlements of the Lowland zone seem to have fallen on evil times, the opposite is true in the Highlands. Here, especially in Wales, where garrisons were weak and the hilltop settlements strong, a vigorous population thrived, independent both of Roman life and Roman interference.

A few isolated large farms of the Roman period have been discovered, purely native in plan, which seem to be "Villas" which were never Romanised, and there are some odd settlements in caves which are difficult to classify. These latter, mostly in limestone areas, sometimes housed surprisingly Romanised inhabitants. Caves in Yorkshire and the Peak District inhabited throughout the period have produced coins and pottery, while Wookey Hole in the Mendips shows a much denser population in the late fourth century when villages were being abandoned. Caves on the coast near Torquay were also occupied at this time, and may have been the refuges of dispossessed villagers.

ROADS

There were two road systems in Roman Britain. Of the first, the main arterial roads which linked the towns and forts, we have an almost complete map, for the solidity of their construction made them a lasting feature of our countryside. Of the second, the minor roads built and maintained by local communities for their own use, we know very little, though thriving groups of Villas well away from main roads show that they must have existed. Ancient tracks along the ridgeways

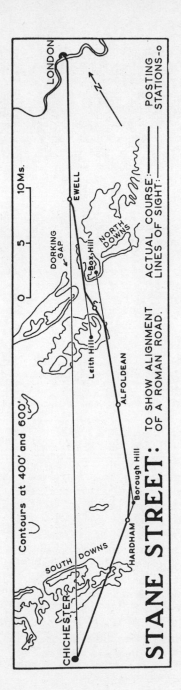

STANE STREET: TO SHOW ALIGNMENT OF A ROMAN ROAD.

ACTUAL COURSE:
LINES OF SIGHT:

POSTING STATIONS — o

Contours at 400' and 600'

were still used by the native population.

The main roads, which form nearly all the 5,000 miles traceable today, were designed for army and government purposes, and the most important were laid down in the actual process of conquest.

The Roman surveyor was quite capable of laying a direct alignment across higher borough to bring the road over the South intervening ridges, and in fact did so in Downs by an easier route and allow use this case from Southwark to the East of the Dorking Gap. From Borough Hill Gate of Chichester: but to follow this a fresh alignment was laid to Box Hill, throughout would have involved unneces- and this was followed up to Holmwood. sary gradients. The road was therefore The two sections were then connected built on this line only as far as Ewell, through the Gap by short straight and another line was laid out from stretches. Chichester to Borough Hill near Pul-

39

Their line was sited from convenient hill-tops along the route, and their construction was the work of military engineers. The method of building varied greatly with the country they had to traverse. A marshy soil or one liable to flooding required a raised causeway, perhaps on a foundation of logs or piles, and even where this was unnecessary the road was generally raised slightly and flanked by ditches for drainage. A lower layer of large stones, and a surface of rammed gravel, were common (though flagstone paving was sometimes employed) and kerbstones were normal. In mountain areas, however, where the way lay over bare hillsides, it was often sufficient to level a terrace in the rock.

The Legionary engineers were more concerned with the rapid movements of troops than with the difficulties of civilian traffic, and their gradients are sometimes very steep by modern standards. Even where they had to take a slope more easily, they preferred to use zig-zags rather than curves.

Apart from troop movements, the main roads served the "Imperial Post" by which Government communications and officials traversed the Province. This was not open to the public like our modern service: it was similar to the government post of Tudor times, which developed into the modern Royal Mail after private persons were allowed to use its facilities.

In civil districts, Posting Stations at distances of twenty to twenty-five miles provided changes of horses for the posting carriages, and accommodation for officials and private travellers in their inns. Where traffic was brisk shops appeared, and bath-houses, and small towns developed.

In the military districts of the Highland zone, however, they are not found: here forts supplied the necessary service.

The roads of Britain were part of the great network which covered the whole Empire, and which made possible the control of remote provinces from a distant centre. They were also the arteries of trade in the civil zone, and an essential part of the defence organisation of the Highlands.

INDUSTRY AND TRADE

The most widespread, and probably the most important, occupation in Roman Britain (apart from agriculture) was mining. Lead especially, from Derbyshire, the Mendips, and elsewhere, was sought after because of the silver which it contained and its many uses as a rustless metal. As a government monopoly, the leadmines in military areas were controlled by the Army and elsewhere by the Procurator (or by private capitalists to whom he leased the rights). The stamped pigs passed down the roads to the Channel ports and thence to Gaul, forming one of the chief British exports.

Tin, which had been mined in Cornwall long before Roman times, was less important. Little effort was made to extract it till the middle of the third century, when the Government's pressing need for revenue caused a sudden revival. Milestones of this period in Cornwall show that roads were built, though their lines have never been traced, and coins became common in areas previously neglected.

Iron was worked in many places, but principally in the Weald of Sussex and the Forest of Dean. The workings were extensive but individually small, and there

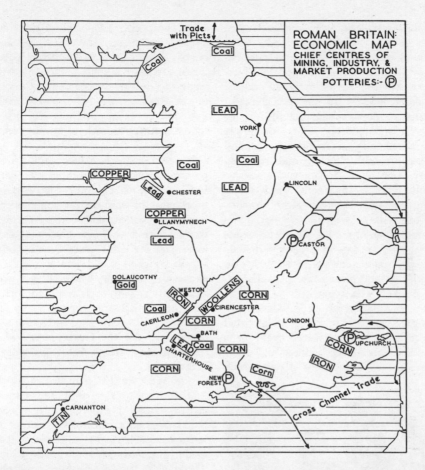

ROMAN BRITAIN:
ECONOMIC MAP
CHIEF CENTRES OF
MINING, INDUSTRY, &
MARKET PRODUCTION
POTTERIES:- Ⓟ

is no sign that they were run by the State. The industry seems to have remained in the hands of the small-scale British workers who had been active before the Romans came. Their methods were not very efficient, and slag-heaps of this period contain so much unextracted iron that some have been re-smelted in modern times. A road of the Roman period from London in the direction of Lewes has been found metalled with iron-slag.

Coal too was raised in many places where it was easily reached in outcrops or by small shafts. This also was a matter of small-scale private workings, and the men who hewed it probably hawked it round about on pack animals as they were still doing two centuries ago. Stores of it found on Hadrian's Wall, however, suggest that the Army may have organised its own supply; and Somerset coal fed the sacred fire of the Temple of Sulis at Bath.

41

Copper was mined to a small extent in Shropshire and North Wales, and there was a Roman gold-mine (with pit-head baths) at Dolaucothy in Carmarthenshire.

A most important industry, and one of particular interest to the archaeologist because of the indestructibility of its product, was pottery. Pots are easily broken, but their pieces last for ever; and Roman Britain both made and imported plenty. Apart from the fine and expensive Samian ware brought over from Gaul, Britain had native potters working as they had long done all over the country. During the Roman period, however, some centres predominate in large-scale manufacture, in particular the Nene Valley on the edge of the Fens and the New Forest. The former was organised by wealthy master-manufacturers, and the latter run by a great number of independent small potters, but both produced ware of a distinctly Roman type. These and other centres turned out masses of pots which were cheap and well-made, if not particularly beautiful, and their products ousted those of the earlier village potter. Their success was such, in fact, that when trade and industry broke down at the end of the Roman period there were hardly any local craftsmen left, and the Britons found themselves without any pottery at all.

Another industry which grew in importance during Roman times was that of wool and woollen cloth. The domestic production of woollens for home use had been long established, but in the later Roman period we find it developing on an industrial scale for market and export. Whole wings of Villas were devoted to it, and in all probability whole villages swept away for sheep-runs. It required apparatus, and therefore capital: only the wealthy Villa-owners could afford to invest in it, or the Government, which seems to have had a weaving factory at Winchester.

Transport was easier in Roman Britain than at any later time until the nineteenth century. Road transport by cart or pack-horse, and boat traffic in rivers deeper and more navigable than at the present day,* made the movement of goods simple. Trade, as in the Middle Ages, took place in three main forms: in the shops and market place of the county town, in country fairs, and by individual peddling. Town markets dwindled in course of time with the decline of the towns themselves, but trade continued if anything more vigorously in rural fairs where Villa-owners who were still prospering could sell their produce and supply their needs. The failure of town life in Britain did not

Potter.

*For canals, see Appendix III, p. 64.

42

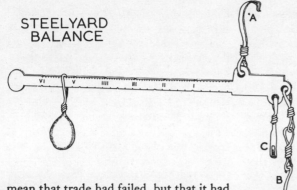

STEELYARD BALANCE

To weigh up to six pounds, the balance was held by the hook A and the object to be weighed suspended from hook B. The weight was then moved along until the arm was horizontal. Objects from six to thirty pounds could be weighed by reversing the apparatus and holding it by the hook C. Roman pounds contained twelve ounces.

mean that trade had failed, but that it had by-passed the dying town for places convenient to the still-thriving Villas.

RELIGION

The religious thought of the Ancient World was not based on the idea of a single Supreme Creator. This had already been evolved by the Jews, from whom Christians (and later Muslims) derived it, but the Jews had been dispersed and the Christians throughout most of the Occupation were a persecuted minority.

Any worship which did not threaten the Government's authority (as Judaism and Druidism did, and Christianity was thought to do) was free to flourish, and one man might worship several gods. In Britain, as throughout the Empire, all were expected to take part in the official Emperor-Worship, but this was little more than a formal sign of loyalty. It was the Christians' refusal of it as idolatrous that led to much of the suspicion against them. Apart from this a man was free to worship as he chose, and he had a great variety to choose from.

Of the old Roman gods, Jupiter was officially worshipped in the Army, but Mars had a more enthusiastic and personal following. Mercury, Hercules, Neptune, Apollo, Minerva, and Diana all found devotees among soldiers and officials, as did Vulcan among the blacksmiths of the Army. But these deities meant little to the Britons, and Cogidubnus's temple to Neptune and Minerva found few imitators.

Besides her own gods, Rome imported those of Egypt, Syria, and the lands beyond her eastern border; and these mostly involved "mystery" cults in which weird things were done in secret and the worshipper passed through successive grades of initiation. These had a considerable appeal to many in search of a personal religion, but they seem to have made no impression on the British population. Isis, Cybele, and the rest were honoured only in the Army or in places like London with a large non-British element.

Instead of the British adopting Roman worship, it was rather the reverse. The Romans had great respect for what they called the *Genius Loci* (spirit of the locality) and when they were long settled

43

in a place they liked to come to terms with the native deities. In the Highland zone the troops joined, as each individual chose, in local worship, and the Celtic deities assumed half-Roman names. Such were "Brigantia", the protector of the Brigantes, and Coventina, in whose little temple on the Wall coins were thrown into a sacred well. In the Lowlands, where there was little non-British population, it is only at cosmopolitan Bath that we know this to have happened. Here the Celtic goddess Sulis received a Roman-style temple in the first century.

The Britons retained their own gods (apart from the Druidism which Rome had smashed) but the process of Romanisation had its effects here too. Small temples of "Romano-Celtic" type are found in the towns and countryside of the Lowland zone, whose construction is Roman but whose plan is confined to the Celtic provinces of the Empire. These little buildings, with their single *cella* for sacrifices, remind us that worship was not congregational and that devotees attended the temple individually to make their offerings and requests. Temples of the classical Graeco-Roman plan are rare in Britain: apart from that of Sulis at Bath, the only example known is the early Temple of Claudius in the Colonia of Colchester.

One imported cult deserves special mention, because it was at one time a serious rival to Christianity. This was the worship of Mithras, a Sun-God of Persian origin, imported into the Empire by troops from the eastern borders and widely followed by soldiers. Unlike most pagan cults it had some moral doctrines, and represented Mithras as Creator and Redeemer, standing for Good against Evil. It had ceremonies closely resembling baptism, confirmation, and communion, and observed 25th December as the "birthday of the Sun" and Sunday as a holy day. Its temples were generally underground, and their "altar piece" was a carving of Mithras slaying a bull, accompanied by the symbolic figures of a dog, a snake, and a scorpion. On either side were two carved figures, one holding a lighted and the other an extinguished torch, re-

ROMANO-CELTIC TEMPLE

Elevation:

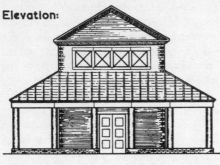

Plan:

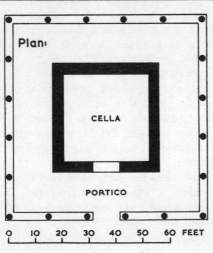

CELLA

PORTICO

0   10   20   30   40   50   60 FEET

presenting Light and Darkness. Mithraism was widespread in Army areas, and the recent discovery of a Mithraeum at London shows that it also flourished among the mixed population of the capital, but it made no impression on the Britons at large.

CHRISTIANITY

The only imported religion which made serious headway amongst the native population was Christianity, and for a long time its growth was slow. Of its origins in Britain we know nothing, and not until the fourth century do we begin to hear something definite. The last great persecution, that of Diocletian's time, caused the martyrdom of St. Alban at Verulamium and of Aaron and Julius of Caerleon; and soon afterwards, when Constantine came to power and the trouble blew over, we find three Bishops from Britain attending a Council at Arles in Gaul in 314. London and York, as we should expect, were represented, and the third was probably from Lincoln. Later in 360 it is recorded that three British Bishops attended a Council at Rimini in Italy, and that they were so poor that the Imperial Government had to pay their expenses. Probably, by or during the fourth century, each of the larger towns in Lowland Britain had its Bishop; but these towns by this time were poverty-stricken places, and most of the Villa-owners were still pagans. Only at Silchester has an undoubted Christian church been discovered, and it was a tiny place among several pagan temples. Doubtless there were many others, but nothing comparable to the splendid pagan Temple of Nodens at Lydney in Glou-

CHRISTIAN CHURCH
SILCHESTER
RECONSTRUCTION AND PLAN

SCALE OF FEET:-
0   10   20   30   40

A small example of the standard type of Christian church of the fourth century, adapted from the Basilica to give room for congregational worship. Normally the bishop's seat replaced that of the magistrate in the basilican apse, though there was hardly room for this at Silchester.

cestershire which was built soon after 360.

By the latter part of the century, however, Christianity was reaching the wealthier classes. The "Chi-Rho" monogram of the first two letters of the name of Christ has been found in Villas at Chedworth (Glos.), Frampton (Dorset), and Appleshaw in Hampshire, and tombstones show that it was reaching the Army

4

45

too. Britain was backward in this respect (as in so many others) compared with the continental provinces, but this was due to its geographical remoteness and the weakness of its towns.

Yet in the troubles of the fifth century British Christianity burst into sudden vigour, and carried the Faith to Irish and Picts beyond the borders of the Province.

ART

The history of Romano-British art is not a happy one. In many things the Britons could adapt themselves easily to Roman ways, but in art their tradition was quite different. The genius of the pre-Conquest British artists lay in one particular direction—abstract designs based on curved lines. Examples on the backs of metal mirrors show a clarity and confidence quite lacking from their later products in Roman times, when they tried to work in the Graeco-Roman style on representations of the human body. The little wooden-faced figures on Romano-British tombstones are sad affairs, produced by men who felt obliged to follow an alien fashion which held no inspiration for them.

There is one startling exception—the Gorgon's head which decorated the Temple of Sulis at Bath. This still exists, to show what a Celtic artist could do with a subject which gave him a chance to express himself in the curved lines of his own tradition. The Gorgon's head has become that of a man with Celtic beard and moustaches, and the flowing locks radiating in all directions within a circular frame are utterly un-Roman and strikingly effective. Such opportunities seldom offered, and most British artists

The Bath Gorgon.

hacked away resignedly at stiff dough-faced memorial sculptures. Yet the native genius somehow survived, and when Roman influence ceased it flowered again in the Celtic Crosses of Northumbria and Cornwall.

THE DECLINE OF THE TOWNS

In the third century, the Roman Empire went through a series of crises from which it never fully recovered. The armies got out of hand and set up a succession of rival Emperors and pretenders, and between 235 and 284 there were twenty-six Augusti of whom only one died a natural death. In the civil wars of this period the frontiers were weakened, and the first serious barbarian inroads began. Meanwhile, rulers completely dependent on the loyalty of the troops raised even higher taxes from the civil population to increase Army pay. Coinage was debased, and for a time became almost worthless, and everyday life was restricted and burdened.

46

The Army, Legions as well as Auxiliaries, was now recruited from the peasantry of the provinces, and therefore from the least civilised part of the population. The new practice of drawing officers from the ranks, and giving them Civil Service posts when they retired, put civil government likewise in the hands of a class which had no sympathy with the Romanised town-dweller, and led to violence and oppression at the expense of the civilian.

Britain escaped the disorders of the period, but could not avoid their effects; and the first result was the decline of her towns. These had been artificial from the beginning, and depended on the encouragement of the Government: now they became the first targets for its extortion. Town authorities were held personally responsible for collecting the much increased taxes demanded from their districts, and the office of Decurion became a sure road to bankruptcy rather than honour. The wealthy consequently avoided the towns, and preferred the safer seclusion of their Villa estates.

Modern excavations have brought to light striking evidence of urban decay at this period. At Verulamium by the later third century the walls were dilapidated, the Theatre was being pulled down for its materials, and houses were deserted and decaying. At Wroxeter the Forum was burnt down about 300 and never rebuilt. Its columns were left lying in the street, and there was not even enough civic energy left to move them out of the way of the traffic. The larger houses of Silchester, formerly the town seats of tribal notables, were given over to squatters. The general picture is of a poverty-stricken population, the decline of municipal government, and the decay of that civilised city life which had begun so bravely.

The centre of Romanised life, in fact, was no longer the towns but the Villas. Here, as throughout the late Roman Empire, the wealthy escaped the worst effects of taxation and continued to prosper, passing the burden on to a wretched peasantry falling fast into serfdom. The towns were the centres of the early Christian communities, and their desertion by the rich and powerful helps to explain the slowness with which the Faith made its early progress in Britain.

CARAUSIUS AND THE SAXONS

In the late third century Britain felt the first effects of that great western movement of peoples already pressing on the Rhine and Danube frontiers. Pirates from the coasts of Germany and Frisia, finding life in their overcrowded and submerging settlements intolerable, took to the sea in search of plunder from the shipping and coasts of Britain and Gaul.

The Romans had always maintained a naval squadron in the Channel, based on Boulogne and the Kentish ports, and this was now reinforced and put in charge of a sea-dog from the Netherlands called Carausius. He coped successfully with the pirates, but showed reluctance to part with the plunder he recovered. Indeed, he was thought to be deliberately permitting raids in order to seize the booty from the pirates later. When he was outlawed by the Roman Government he landed in Britain, called on the Legions to back him (which they did) and declared himself Emperor in Britain. This was not a national declaration of independence, for the Empire was already partitioned between several rulers, and it would be mistaken to regard him as a second Caratacus. He secured his position by defeating some Auxiliary regiments who opposed him, strengthening his fleet, and beating off an invasion at sea.

This was in 286 or 287, and for some years he ruled in Britain and apparently ruled well. For a time, too, his seapower gave him control of the opposite coast of Gaul, though he lost this in 293. His career was cut short in the same year when his Procurator Allectus murdered him to escape punishment for his crimes, and declared himself Emperor. But no one had much use for Allectus, and in 296 Constantius Chlorus, Caesar of Gaul, was able to defeat him without difficulty and recover Britain. Meanwhile, however, Allectus had stripped the north of its garrisons to defend himself, and the Picts had broken in. Constantius had to repair much damage along the wall, and to rebuild the Legionary fortress at York, where the Multangular Tower still bears witness to his work.

SAXON SHORE FORTS

Rome was now everywhere on the defensive, and part of Constantius's work was to reorganise the defences to meet the new threat by sea. Along the coast from the Wash to the Solent was built a new line of forts on what was now called the "Saxon Shore", in the massive style of late Roman military architecture, and two forts of earlier type at Brancaster and Reculver were included in the system. These forts (see map) were all on the shore-line overlooking harbours, and designed as protected bases for naval patrols as well as for an Auxiliary garrison. Compared with the simple structures of earlier times, their walls were higher, their gates few and small, and they had great projecting bastions for heavy stone-throwing artillery. Unlike earlier forts, they were made to give the maximum advantage to a garrison too weak to meet their enemies in the open. So solid was their concrete that far more remains of some of them today (e.g., at Pevensey and Portchester) than of any forts of an earlier period.

Nor were the Saxons the only seaborne danger. The Irish too were becom-

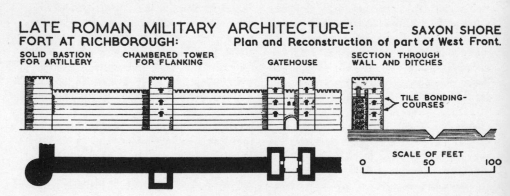

LATE ROMAN MILITARY ARCHITECTURE: SAXON SHORE
FORT AT RICHBOROUGH: Plan and Reconstruction of part of West Front.

SOLID BASTION FOR ARTILLERY CHAMBERED TOWER FOR FLANKING GATEHOUSE SECTION THROUGH WALL AND DITCHES

TILE BONDING-COURSES

SCALE OF FEET
0   50   100

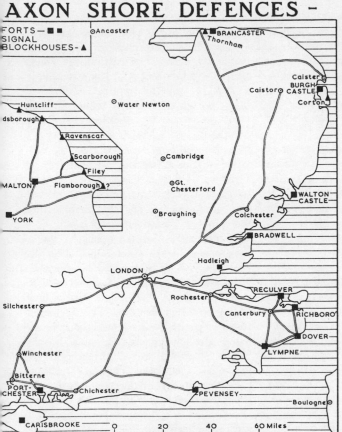

FORTS - ■ ■
SIGNAL
BLOCKHOUSES - ▲

The forts at Brancaster and Reculver were of second century type, and are older than the rest of the chain. The signal station on Flamborough Head almost certainly existed, but any remains have been lost through coast erosion.

ing a menace, and defences in Wales had to be reorganised. About this time the Second Legion finally left its fortress at Caerleon, and moved for a while to a new one of Saxon Shore type at Cardiff (which has been partially reconstructed in modern times). New waterside forts were also built at Caernarvon and Holyhead.

DIOCLETIAN'S REORGANISATION

Diocletian (284–305) rescued the Em-

pire for a time from its third-century chaos, and reorganised it on a new plan. Recognising that one man could no longer control and defend all its vast extent, he divided it between two Augusti of east and west, and each Augustus adopted a Caesar as his assistant and successor. Each of the four had his "Prefecture" with his own Army, capital, and Civil Service, and each Prefecture was subdivided into Dioceses and Provinces. Much effort was made to prevent men running away from their responsibilities and burdens, and to compel the leading men of the Civitates to live in their towns and take office. The peasantry were legally bound to the soil, and the craftsmen to their place of work, and laws did whatever laws could do to stabilize life and keep the machine of taxation and government running.

Britain became a Diocese, under a Vicarius or viceroy, and was divided into four small Provinces known as Britannia Prima, Britannia Secunda, Flavia Caesariensis, and Maxima Caesariensis. Apart from the fact that Cirencester was in Britannia Prima, we know nothing of their boundaries. The Army was reorganised under a Duke of Britain (Dux Britanniarum) with headquarters at York, in charge of the frontier garrisons, and later a Count of Britain (Comes) commanding a field army. The southeastern forts and fleet were under the separate control of the Count of the Saxon Shore. Some effort seems to have been made to get the towns on their feet again, for the walls of Verulamium were repaired at this time, its Theatre rebuilt, and houses built or reconstructed. It was a failure, however; within fifty years the Theatre was a rubbish dump, and only a miserable squatter population was left in the decaying houses.

This reorganisation was an attempt to deal, by harsh measures, with the symptoms of the diseases from which the Empire was suffering: it failed to remove the root causes of over-taxation, concentration of wealth in the hands of a few, and oppression of the civil population by the Army and the government officials.

It was not long before external pressure on the decaying Empire led to an increasingly desperate situation, in which Britain was involved with the rest About 340 we find Scots from Ireland filtering into the western regions where Roman troops were too few to keep them out, and the Government confessing its weakness by recognising them as "Allies" (*Foederati*) in an attempt to pacify them with words for lack of force. In 360 troops had to be sent from Gaul to drive out barbarian invaders from Britain, but four years later they were back again.

In 368 came a united attack by Picts, Saxons and Scots, which submerged the defences. Helped by treachery in the now half-barbarised garrison, the Picts swept over Hadrian's Wall while Scots and Saxons invaded by sea. The Duke of Britain and the Count of the Saxon Shore fell in the general disaster, and the invaders swarmed across the country—probably joined, as in Gaul, by rebellious peasants who hated their own landlords and Government more than the outsider and had nothing to lose. Many Villas must have been sacked in the turmoil; but the town walls, manned by refugees from the countryside, proved able to keep out hordes not equipped for sieges. Most of the towns by now were hardly worth plundering anyway.

When the Emperor Valentinian sent Count Theodosius to deal with the situation, he landed to find Kent terrorised by robber bands and the Londoners cowering behind closed gates. Once more order was restored and the Wall reoccupied, but the patrolling troops of the milecastles (who may have been involved

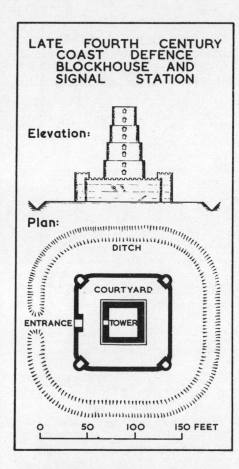

LATE FOURTH CENTURY COAST DEFENCE BLOCKHOUSE AND SIGNAL STATION

Elevation:

Plan:

DITCH

COURTYARD

ENTRANCE   TOWER

0   50   100   150 FEET

bastions able to mount light artillery. Another signal station of this period has been found on the south shore of the Bristol Channel, and there may have been many others which have disappeared with cliff-erosion. There is no sign of the Twentieth Legion in its fortress at Chester after 367; and since there were far more troops at Caernarvon between this date and 383, it is possible it was moved there to face the Irish.

London now received the honourable name of "Augusta" (though it never replaced "Londinium") and a new province of Valentia was organised which probably included the Foederati of Wales.

THE END OF ROMAN OCCUPATION

The final collapse of the defences of Roman Britain was due more to troubles within the Empire, and the invasion of the continental provinces, than to the pressure of Picts and Saxons. In 383 the best part of the troops were carried off to Gaul by their commander Maximus, who declared himself Emperor, and as a result Hadrian's Wall was finally overrun and lost. After some successes, Maximus fell in 388; and about 395 the new signal-stations of the Yorkshire coast were stormed and left littered with the bodies of their defenders.

The christianised Vandal Stilicho, who made a gallant effort to hold up the tottering Empire, again reorganised the defences of Britain at the end of the fourth century, but on a contracted scale. Troops could no longer be found to garrison all the forts of the Uplands, and the new line was drawn in an attempt to protect the civilised Lowlands only. The Second Legion was moved to its last quarters at

in the original treachery) were not replaced. The Saxons were now evidently venturesome enough to make the longer crossing to Yorkshire, and a line of massively-built signal stations was erected to warn a squadron in the Humber of their approach. These consisted of a central tower, with walls eight feet thick at the base and five feet or more above, and rising perhaps as much as 100 feet, surrounded by a curtain wall with small

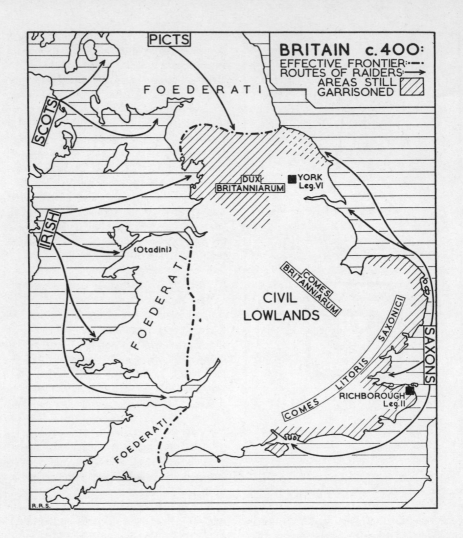

Richborough to stiffen the Saxon Shore defences, and Wales and the north were left in charge of Foederati. About 400 an entire tribe of these, the Otadini under their chief Cunedda, were moved from the Wall district to North Wales to meet the Irish danger.

The Gothic invasion of the heart of the Empire caused Stilicho to withdraw much of the remaining troops in 402, and it is unlikely that they ever returned. After this the few remaining regiments, feeling themselves abandoned, set up a series of short-lived "Emperors" to give them the leadership which could no longer come from Rome. One of these again took troops out of the country in an attempt to hold Gaul, and the Britons disowned him and appealed direct to the Emperor Honorius for help. This was in 410, when Alaric's Goths were on the point of sacking Rome itself, and Honorius could spare nothing. Shortly before the City fell he addressed his famous *Rescript* to the Civitates of Britain, telling them to make their own arrangements for the defence and government of the province.

No one regarded this as more than a temporary measure: the idea of the permanence and necessity of the Empire was so deeply embedded in men's minds that its final collapse was unthinkable. For years the vanished garrisons of Hadrian's Wall remained in the Roman Army lists, ready to be replaced when circumstances allowed, and a brief re-occupation of the south-east may actually have taken place for some years after 417. At Richborough in particular great quantities of late coinage have been found, suggesting the payment of troops, and other south-eastern sites show similar evidence. But when St. Germanus visited Britain in 429 and led Britons to victory over barbarian raiders, there seem to have been no regular troops left in the island.

SUB-ROMAN BRITAIN

The withdrawal of Roman troops and government was not the end of Roman Britain. It seems, curiously, to have coincided with the dying away of Irish and Pictish raiding, and for a time the local British authorities contrived to keep some sort of government going and even to strike coins. The towns were not sacked in the troubles of the last phase of occupation, and they may even have enjoyed some temporary revival. Their walls must have attracted refugees, especially from the more Romanised part of the population, though the breakdown of trade and the ravaging of the countryside can have left them little beyond a hand-to-mouth existence.

Villas, lying in the open, had no doubt been pillaged, and many finally destroyed, but the land was indestructible; and where there were survivors they may have patched up the damage and kept life going. The lack of coins in them after the late fourth century is evidence for impoverishment, but not necessarily for desertion: life on the land could still go on without cash, though also without the comforts and refinements which they had formerly enjoyed. St. Patrick's home was raided by Irish pirates early in the fifth century, and he and his sisters carried off, but he found the family still living there when he returned many years later.

The "Departure of the Romans", in fact, meant that of troops and officials, and perhaps merchants, but it left behind the great bulk of that part of the British population who regarded themselves as equally "Roman". The people of towns and villas did not give up their civilised way of life without a bitter struggle against increasingly difficult conditions.

Though Irish and Picts ceased from troubling, the Saxons were an increasing menace; and against them the British needed leadership. This the Romanised class failed to provide. The methods of the late Roman government had crushed the spirit of the leaders of the Civitates and deprived them of power, and it was the

EARLY BRITISH CHRISTIANITY:
FOURTH CENTURY:
KNOWN COMMUNITIES:
PROBABLE COMMUNITIES:
PROBABLE EXTENT OF URBAN-
CENTRED BRITISH CHURCH
OTHER KNOWN SITES:
FIFTH CENTURY:
ROMANO-BRITISH
MISSIONS THUS: NINIAN
RESULTING MONASTIC
CELTIC CHURCH:

NINIAN

CORBRIDGE
CARLISLE
Whithorn
397
BROUGHAM

ARMAGH

PATRICK
KELLS

York

PATRICK

Lincoln

(Chester)

(Wroxeter)
(Leicester)   (Caistor)

ILLTUD

(Colchester)

(Gloucester) CHEDWORTH St. Albans
Caerwent
Caerleon   (Cirencester)   London
                                      LULLINGSTONE
                        Silchester   Canterbury
                    APPLESHAW
                    (Winchester)
                                    (Chichester)
            FRAMPTON
(Exeter)   (Dorchester)

R. R. S.

more vigorous people of the un-Roman-
ised west who took their place. One such
was Vortigern, a ruler in Wales who
made his authority accepted as far as
Kent, and who plays a part in one of the
few well-attested facts of this dim period
of history. With the rise of such crude and
ruthless characters, the Romanised section of the Britons was pushed into the
background: and with the chaos which
followed the Saxon invasions their culture
faded to a wistful memory.

BRITISH CHRISTIAN MISSIONS

Whatever the Romanised class in Britain may have lacked in capacity for leadership, it showed amazing vigour at this period in spreading Christianity to the uncivilised areas formerly occupied only by the Army, and to Ireland where Roman troops had never ventured. The first missionary of note was Ninian, a Romanised Briton of the late fourth century, who studied and took Bishop's Orders in Rome and was a disciple of the monastic pioneer Martin of Tours. By the time he was ready to begin his mission, the troops had withdrawn from the Wall and the north; yet in 397 he struck out far beyond the then frontier to found his monastery at Whithorn in Galloway. From there, until his death in 432, he worked along the Roman roads as far as Glasgow and Aberdeenshire, and across the Solway into Cumberland, converting the southern Picts and the sub-Roman populations which huddled on the sites of deserted forts. To him and his followers was largely due the peculiar monastic organisation of the Celtic Church, which was suited to a land without towns but quite different from that of the Roman provinces centred on the city and its Bishop.

St. Patrick also came from the Romanised part of the population. His father, a Christian deacon, was also a landowner and a Decurion. His birthplace has been generally sought in the north, but since there is some doubt whether Decurions would have existed outside the Lowlands, the Severn Valley has been suggested. At the age of fifteen he was carried off by raiders and sold as a slave in Ireland, where he spent six years before escaping. Determined to bring Christianity to his pagan captors, he first studied in Gaul and was consecrated Bishop. In 432 he began his mission, with the backing of the British Church which sent him helpers, and set out to organise an Irish Church on the British model. But Ireland, like North Britain, had no towns worth mentioning, and his efforts at conversion were more successful than his organisation. After his death in 461 the Irish Church fell under the influence of Ninian's followers from Galloway, and adopted the Celtic idea of the monastery centre and the wandering Bishop.

Meanwhile St. Illtud, who had been a fellow-student with Patrick under St. Germanus, was sending out missionaries from his monastery-school in Glamorgan to found the Faith firmly in the hills of Wales.

Between them these three pioneers spread Christianity over all the "Celtic Fringe" except the Scottish Highlands, at the very time when the civilisation they represented was sinking into ruin.

THE BEGINNINGS OF SAXON SETTLEMENT

Permanent Saxon settlement, as distinct from raiding, seems to have begun about 450 when Vortigern adopted the old Roman device of accepting barbarian bands as *Foederati*. Settled in Thanet in the hope that they would help to keep out others, they served instead as the advance guard of a host. From then onwards for the rest of the fifth century there was infiltration by war-bands into Kent, and into the coastlands and river valleys of the south-east.

The character of these newcomers had

much to do with the extinction of what remained of Roman life in Britain. Unlike the invaders of most of the continental provinces, they had with few exceptions been untouched by Roman civilisation; and since they had to come by sea they arrived in small parties rather than in the organised hosts under powerful leaders which crossed the Rhine. Their conquest therefore was gradual, involving a long period of crisis and disorganisation, and their object was to win land on which to pioneer their own villages instead of to take over and enjoy the towns and villas. In the process they made impossible for the Britons the civilised life for which they themselves had no appreciation.

Most of them came from the North Sea coast of Germany, but a few from Frisia had already been in contact with the Roman frontiers and were exceptional in having some idea of Roman life. These (known as Jutes, though they had long ceased to have any connection with Jutland) occupied Kent, and here we find the invaders adopting the tribal name of the local Britons (Cantiaci) and their county town as a seat of government. Canterbury (Cantwarabyrig) replaced Durovernum Cantiacorum as Paris took its name from Lutetia Parisiorum. Such examples are frequent in Gaul, but there is no other in Britain. In Kent, too, other Roman towns or forts, such as Rochester, Dover, and Lympne, were early occupied as local centres, though no Villa buildings are known to have been taken over. It would be rash, however, to assume that the newcomers adopted Canterbury as a going concern, for Augustine at the end of the next century found no Christians surviving there.

Elsewhere, we can say with confidence that city life, already undermined in the fourth century, ceased by the end of the fifth. Some large towns were simply abandoned, such as Verulamium, Wroxeter, and Silchester, as were most of the small ones. Others continued to shelter a shrunken population of miserable squatters scraping a living from smallholdings or brigandage, but indistinguishable in their way of life from villagers. Only the old Colonia at Lincoln shows any sign of having perhaps preserved more than this: the remarkable survival of its Roman name, the better state of its walls, and the absence of early English settlement in its neighbourhood, may indicate the continuance of some organised life. In general the English invasions, by reducing the life of the countryside to uncertainty and disorder, made it impossible for that of the towns to continue.

Villas also came to an end, either by fire and slaughter or by desertion. Their large-scale agriculture could not carry on when there was no market for their surplus, and the buildings themselves must soon have become impossible to repair for lack of glass and tiles and skilled workmen. Where they escaped outright destruction, they passed through a period of shrinkage and decay, until their isolation proved too dangerous and their last owners decamped to the protection of town walls or a village community. With the stoppage of trade and industrial production, life in the countryside must have soon lost any Roman character and reverted to primitive conditions.

In such troubled times we should expect to find British villages attacked and burnt out, but there is little if any

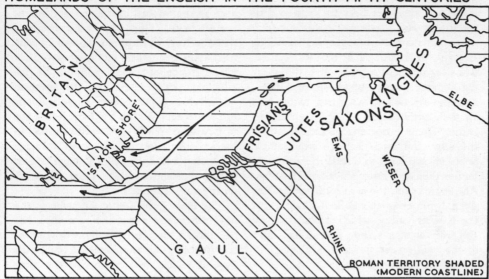

ROMAN TERRITORY SHADED
(MODERN COASTLINE)

evidence that this happened. They were hardly worth looting, and the upland soils on which most of them stood did not attract the invaders. Like the Villas (in this if in nothing else) the Saxons used a heavy plough and preferred to cultivate great open fields—where possible on a fertile clay. The British villages were mostly deserted, in course of time, in the areas the English conquered: but this seems to have come about gradually as the result of absorption into new settlements on the better valley land opened up by Saxon forest-clearing.

In the conquered areas, Christianity practically disappeared. This is less surprising when we realise that the strength of the Romano-British Church lay in the towns and the civilised classes, and that the majority of countryfolk were still pagan when the English came. The flight or extinction of the Romanised population crippled a Church organised round the Bishops of the cities, at the time when the differently-organised Celtic Church was making vigorous progress beyond the reach of the invaders. In 455 the British Church was still in touch with Rome, and able to adopt the changed calculation of Easter made in that year. Thirty years later, when another change was made, a wedge of pagan Saxons had cut off its remnants from the continental Church.

BRITAIN ABOUT 500

By the end of the fifth century the habitable parts of the east coast to the Humber and the south coast to the Solent had been occupied by the English, and settlement stretched far inland up all the important river valleys, into the Upper Thames, the Midlands, and the

57

Vale of York. About this time, however, there seems to have been a check. Out of the myths which have gathered round his name we may disentangle the figure of Artorius or Arthur, a British war leader, who organised a mobile field-force of mail-coated cavalry of late-Roman type, and by a series of victories halted the English advance for a half a century to come. There is nothing incredible about the story, for such a force would have been as superior to crude Saxon foot-tactics then as it later proved at Hastings. About this time too was built the Wansdyke, from near the Bristol Channel to the Kennet Valley, which was apparently the frontier of a strong British kingdom of the south-west facing the English of the Upper Thames Basin.

Wales and the Severn Valley were still in British hands, as were the Pennines and the uplands of the North. North of Thames, the Chiltern forests seem to have been still under British control, and so quite possibly was Lincoln. But nearly all of what had been the most civilised part of the Roman province was now subject to the English, and in that fact we see the real end of Roman Britain.

Many British, of course, survived in the conquered areas, and here and there little pockets may have maintained a precarious independence. Most, however, must have come to terms with the invaders and accepted a situation they could not prevent. One striking fact in the modern map of England is that outside Wales and Cornwall British village-names have almost vanished, even in western districts where survival was greatest. This has been used to argue that the Britons were nearly exterminated, but the allied fact that British names for hills and rivers predominate even in the far east of the country proves the opposite. It can hardly be imagined that the English inquired the name of the local river from their victims before they wiped them out. The loss of British village names, in fact, shows the desertion of the villages but not the disappearance of the Britons. As the English cleared the forests and made new settlements on better soils, the British seem to have gradually left their windy heights and joined the new valley communities as partners or dependents.

The loss of the Celtic language in the lowlands is also a fact of importance, but this too no more proves the extinction of the Britons than the fact that the Gauls gave up Celtic for Latin proves that they had ceased to exist. In both cases a conquered people adopted the language of the conqueror. The permeation of Lowland Britain was a long slow process, and even the Laws of Alfred (late ninth century) refer to Welshmen as a distinct part of Wessex society, ranging in status from serfs to considerable landowners.

In Wales, of course, and to a less extent in Cornwall, the vigorous race which already contrasted in Roman times with the depressed villagers of the Lowlands continued to flourish, and to maintain its independence, its Celtic tongue, and its new-found Christianity. Its learned men could still write Latin, though this accomplishment was rare even among churchmen. But of its Roman heritage it kept little but the "glory of an ancient name".

CONCLUSION

Up to the fifth century, the history of Britain is closely linked with that of Gaul.

BRITAIN IN THE EARLY SIXTH CENTURY
APPROXIMATE EXTENT OF ENGLISH PENETRATION & SETTLEMENT:
OVER 1000'

Both contain a Celtic population, of a similar way of life; both become Roman provinces, and both are (in different degrees) Romanised.

But here the parallel ends. The great differences which distinguish later England and France have their roots in the period of Roman Occupation, and their chief cause in the conditions of the respective barbarian conquests. Britain was never as fully Romanised as Gaul: its towns were never so large or well established, and its countryside, outside the Villas, was much less influenced by Roman ways. In Gaul, Latin (or a simplified version) became the language of

59

the peasantry, while in Britain it was confined to a small Romanised class.

Gaul, too, was invaded by a Frankish host which had long been in contact with Rome, and whose object was to replace the existing rulers and landowners. As a large organised force they were able to make a quick conquest, which caused far less dislocation, and having done this they regarded the towns and Villas as assets to be enjoyed. In France, Villas survived to give their names to many modern villages: and towns preserved an unbroken life as the Bishop took over when the imperial officials failed. The Franks, as a ruling minority, were in due course absorbed as the Normans were in England: they learnt the language and religion of the conquered.

In England, the opposite occurred. The conquered population was less numerous in proportion to its conquerors, and its civilised elements went under instead of remaining to lead it and civilise the invader. The English, unlike the Franks, conquered piecemeal and in complete disregard of the civilisation they found. Their object was only to reproduce, in better conditions, the simple village life to which they were accustomed.

The Roman period, which is basic to the history of France, is an interlude in that of Britain. Of its effects on ideas, institutions, and way of life, scarcely a trace remained (except the Celtic Church, which was rather a by-product than a direct result). Yet it was not without its influence on later events. The roads it left behind it were through centuries the only ones worthy of the name, and many have remained in unbroken use to the present day. Town walls too remained, though the life of which they were a symbol vanished, and in due course they and the roads leading to them caused a re-occupation of nearly all Roman town sites. It is no coincidence that most of our ancient cathedral cities are of Roman origin (though many did not get their Bishops till Norman times or later) and that most of our important towns before the Industrial Revolution grew up at places first chosen by the Romans.

Rome gave much to the stream of English life, but apart from her roads and town sites she gave it indirectly and long after the Roman Empire and its British province had ceased to be.

THE PLACE-NAMES OF ROMAN BRITAIN

Our knowledge of Romano-British place-names is derived from road-books, army lists, and inscriptions. Nearly all are Latin forms of native Celtic names, though a few are purely Roman (e.g., Pons Aelii ("Hadrian's Bridge"), Pontes ("Bridges" or "The Great Bridge") and Aquae ("Waters" or "Spa")). Tribal capitals sometimes have the tribal name (in its Latin genitive plural) added. The main roads very probably had Latin names, but these are unknown. Some maps show road names which are the inventions of later antiquaries, as are some suggested place-names. Those which can be identified with certainty or near-certainty are as follows:

TOWNS AND CIVIL SETTLEMENTS

Abone—Sea Mills (near Bristol)

Ad Pontem—East Stoke (on Trent)

Aquae Arnemetiae—Buxton

Aquae Sulis—Bath

Ariconium—Weston under Penyard (near Ross)

Bannaventa—Whilton (near Daventry)

Bravonium—Leintwardine (near Ludlow)

Caesaromagus—Chelmsford

Calleva (Atrebatum)—Silchester

Camulodunum—Colchester

Causennae—Ancaster (Lincs.)

Clausentum—Bitterne (near Southampton)

Condate—Northwich (Cheshire)

Corinium (Dobunorum)—Cirencester

Corstopitum—Corbridge

Crococalana—Brough (near Lincoln)

Cunetio—Mildenhall (near Marlborough)

Danum—Doncaster

Durnovaria—Dorchester (Dorset)

Durobrivae—Castor (on Nene) and Rochester

Durocobrivae—Dunstable

Durovernum (Cantiacorum)—Canterbury

Glevum—Gloucester

Isca (Dumnoniorum)—Exeter

Isurium (Brigantium)—Aldborough (Yorks.)

Lactodorum—Towcester

Letocetum—Wall (Staffs.)

Lindinae—Ilchester

Lindum Colonia—Lincoln

Londinium (Augusta)—London

Luguvallium—Carlisle

Magiovinium—Little Brickhill (near Bletchley)

Magnis—Kenchester (near Hereford)

Manduessedum—Mancetter (near Nuneaton)

Nidum—Neath

Noviomagus (Regnensium)—Chichester

Pennocrucium—Penkridge (Staffs.)

Petuaria—Brough on Humber

Pontes—Staines

Ratae (Coritanorum)—Leicester

Salinae—Droitwich

Sorbiodunum—Old Sarum (near Salisbury)

Spinae—Speen (near Newbury)

Sulloniacae—Brockley Hill (near Watford)

Uxacona—Oakengates (near Wellington, Salop)

Vaginacae—Springhead (near Gravesend)

Venonae—(junction of Fosse Way and Watling Street)

Venta (Belgarum)—Winchester

Venta (Icenorum)—Caistor (near Norwich)

Venta (Silurum)—Caerwent

Verlucio—Sandy Lane (N. Wilts.)

Vernemetum—Willoughby (Notts.)

Verulamium—St. Albans

Vindogladia—Woodyates (E. Dorset)

Viroconium (Cornoviorum)—Wroxeter

(some with attached civil settlements)

Aballava—Papcastle (near Cockermouth)
Aesica—Great Chesters (Hadrian's Wall)
Alone—Watercrook (near Kendal)
Anavio—Brough (Derbyshire)
Anderida—Pevensey (Sussex)

Banna—Bewcastle (Cumb.)
Blatobulgium—Birrens (Dumfries)
Borcovicium—Housesteads (Hadrian's Wall)
Branodunum—Brancaster (Norfolk)
Bravoniacum—Kirby Thore (near Appleby)
Bremenium—High Rochester (Northumb.)
Bremetennacum—Ribchester (near Preston)
Brocavum—Brougham (near Penrith)
Burrium—Usk (Mon.)

Calcaria—Tadcaster
Camboglanna—Birdoswald (Hadrian's Wall)
Canovium—Caerhun (near Conway)
Castra Exploratorum—Netherby (near Carlisle)
Cataractonium—Catterick (Yorks.)
Cilurnum—Chesters (Hadrian's Wall)
Clanoventa—Ravenglass (Cumb.)
Coccium—Wigan
Condercum—Benwell (Hadrian's Wall)

Derventio—Malton (Yorks.)
Deva—Chester
Dubris—Dover

Eburacum—York

Galava—Ambleside (Westm.)
Gariannonum—Burgh Castle (near Yarmouth)
Gobannium—Abergavenny

Habitancum—Risingham (Northumb.)

Hunnum—Halton (Hadrian's Wall)

Isca—Caerleon

Lavatrae—Bowes (N. Riding)
Legeolium—Castleford (near Pontefract)
Lemanis—Lympne
Leucarum—Loughor (near Swansea)
Longovicium—Lanchester (Durham)

Magnis—Carvoran (Hadrian's Wall)
Mamucium—Manchester
Margidunum—(near Bingham, Notts.)
Maridunum—Caermarthen

Olicana—Ilkley
Othona—Bradwell (Essex)

Petrianae—Old Carlisle (near Wigton, Cumb.)
Pons Aelii—Newcastle
Portus Adurni—Portchester
Procolitia—Carrawburgh (Hadrian's Wall)

Regulbium—Reculver (Kent)
Rutupiae—Richborough

Segedunum—Wallsend
Segontium—Caernarvon

Trimontium—Newstead (on Tweed)

Uxellodunum—Castlesteads (Hadrian's Wall)
Uxellodunum—Maryport (Cumb.)

Varae—St. Asaph (N. Wales)
Verterae—Brough (Cumb.)
Vindobala—Rudchester (Hadrian's Wall)
Vindolanda—Chesterholm (Hadrian's Wall)
Vindomora—Ebchester (Durham)
Vinovia—Binchester (near Bishop Auckland)
Voreda—Old Penrith (Cumb.)

ROMAN EMPERORS, AND GOVERNORS OF BRITAIN DURING THE FORMATIVE PERIOD

EMPEROR	GOVERNOR
Claudius 41–54	Aulus Plautius 43–47
	Ostorius Scapula 47–52
Nero 54–68	Didius Gallus 52–58
	Veranius Nepos 58–59
	Suetonius Paulinus 59–61
	Petronius Turpilianus 61–63
Vespasian 69–79 ⎱	Trebellius Maximus 63–69
Titus 71–81 ⎰	Vettius Bolanus 69–71
	Petillius Cerealis 71–74
	Julius Frontinus 74–78
Domitian 81–96	Julius Agricola 78–85
	Sallustius Lucullus (?)
	Metilius Nepos 98
Trajan 98–117	Avidius Quietus 98–101
	Neratius Marcellus 101–103
Hadrian 117–138	Pompeius Falco 118–122
	Platorius Nepos 122–126
	Julius Severus 130–134
Antoninus Pius 138–161	Lollius Urbicus 138–144
	Julius Verus 155–160
	Statius Priscus 160–161
Marcus Aurelius 161–180	Calpurnius Agricola 161–165
	Ulpius Marcellus 175–180, 184–185
Commodus 180–192	Helvius Pertinax 185
Severus 193–211	Clodius Albinus 196
	Virius Lupus 197–200
	Pollenius Auspex
	Alfenus Senecio 209

THE ROMAN CANAL SYSTEM OF THE FENLANDS

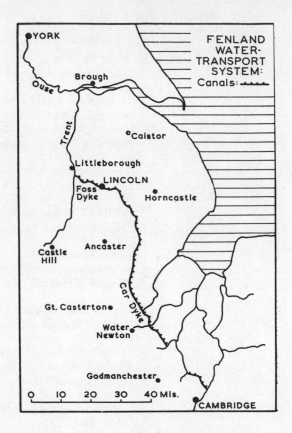

The revolt of the Iceni in A.D. 61 gave the Roman government an opportunity to use the forced labour of the defeated rebels for large schemes of land reclamation and settlement in the Fenlands. Much of the corn produced here was needed for the Ninth Legion at Lincoln; and since it could be more easily moved by water than by road, a canal system which served for transport as well as drainage was built to link all the major Fenland rivers with that city. After the legion moved to York, the Foss Dyke was cut between Lincoln and the Trent to give through communication by way of the Humber and Ouse to the new military base.

A Select Book List

REVISED BY NORMAN STONE, A.L.A.
(See also the book list of *Ancient Rome*, by Duncan Taylor)

BRITISH MUSEUM. *A Guide to the Antiquities of Roman Britain.* British Museum, repr. 1953. Illus. A survey of the antiquities preserved in the Department of British and Medieval Antiquities illustrative of the life and art of the period.

BRUCE, J. COLLINGWOOD. *Handbook to the Roman Wall*, edited by Ian A. Richmond. Reid, 11th ed. 1956. Illus., map, book list. A pocket guide and reference book.

BURN, A. R. *Agricola and Roman Britain.* English Universities Press ("Teach Yourself History" Series), 1953. Book list. A biography of Julius Agricola, Governor of Britain, with an account of his campaigns and of the political and social background to the period.

BURN, A. R. *The Romans in Britain: an Anthology of Inscriptions.* Blackwell, 1932. A handy introduction to the inscriptions of Roman Britain.

COLLINGWOOD, R. G. *Roman Britain.* Oxford, rev. ed. repr. 1953. Illus., book list. A general sketch of Roman Britain, well illustrated.

COLLINGWOOD, R. G. *and* MYRES, J. N. L. *Roman Britain and the English Settlements.* Oxford, 2nd ed. repr. 1945. Book list. Vol. I of "The Oxford History of England". A detailed survey of Roman rule in Britain and its effect on the state of the country and the people. Advanced study.

COTTRELL, LEONARD. *Seeing Roman Britain.* Evans, 1956. Illus., maps, tables. A personal account of travels in search of Roman Britain. Contains a useful list of museums which exhibit Roman-British specimens.

DURANT, G. M. *Journey into Roman Britain.* Bell, 1957. Illus., maps, plans. An introduction designed for the interested traveller.

HAWKES, JACQUETTA. *A Guide to the Prehistoric and Roman Monuments in England and Wales*. Chatto and Windus, 1951. Illus., maps. Contains a gazetteer.

LINDSAY, JACK. *The Romans were Here: the Roman Period in Britain and its Place in our History*. Muller, 1956. Illus., map, book list. A good introduction for the layman.

MARGARY, I. D. *Roman Roads in Britain*. 2 vols. Phoenix, 1955–57. Illus. A comprehensive survey.

MOORE, R. W. *The Romans in Britain: a Selection of Latin Texts, edited with a commentary*. Methuen, 3rd ed. rev. by W. W. Ward, 1954. Illus., book list. An introduction to the study of Roman Britain, intended for use in schools where Latin is taught.

QUENNELL, M. *and* C. H. B. *Everyday Life in Roman Britain*. Batsford, 3rd ed. rev. 1952. Illus. A study of life in Britain during the Roman occupation, covering social and domestic matters, the army and travel, roads and towns, and the Roman character and rule.

RICHMOND, IAN A. *Roman Britain*. Penguin, 1955. Illus., book list. Vol. I of "The Pelican History of England". A general picture of the Roman invasion and occupation of Britain from A.D. 43 to the fifth century, embodying recent ideas and discoveries. A revised edition will be published in 1963 by Cape.

FICTION

PLOWMAN, STEPHANIE. *To Spare the Conquered*. Methuen, 1960.

SUTCLIFF, ROSEMARY. *The Eagle of the Ninth*. Oxford, 1954. Illus.

SUTCLIFF, ROSEMARY. *Outcast*. Oxford, 1955. Illus.

TREASE, GEOFFREY. *Word to Caesar*. Macmillan, 1955. Illus.

TREECE, HENRY. *Legions of the Eagle*. Bodley Head, 1954. Illus.

Junior historical novels giving a picture of life in Britain under the Romans.

Index